CANADIAN GHOST STORIES

Volume II

Susan Smitten
Edrick Thay
Dale Jarvis
Vernon Oickle

GHOST
HOUSE

Ghost House Books

The Publisher: Ghost House Books
Distributed by Lone Pine Publishing
10145–81 Avenue
Edmonton, AB T6E 1W9
Canada

Website: http://www.ghostbooks.net

National Library of Canada Cataloguing in Publication Data
Canadian ghost stories, volume II / Susan Smitten... [et al.].

ISBN 1-894877-24-1

1. Ghosts—Canada. 2. Legends—Canada. I. Smitten, Susan, 1961–
GR580.C36 2003   398.2'097105   C2003-910941-0

Editorial Director: Nancy Foulds
Project Editor: Faye Boer
Illustrations Coordinator: Carol Woo
Production Manager: Gene Longson
Cover Design: Gerry Dotto
Book Design, Layout & Production: Lynett McKell
Photo Credits: Every effort has been made to accurately credit photographers. Any errors or
omissions should be directed to the publisher for changes in future editions. The photo-
graphs and illustrations in this book are reproduced with the kind permission of the fol-
lowing sources: Bytown Museum (p. 12), Archives of Ontario (p. 10, 18, 45, 53), Centre for
Addiction and Mental Health Archives, University of Toronto (p. 49), Ken Sooley (p. 61,
63), iStock/Barbara Henry (p. 67, 87), iStock/Gray Goodfleisch (p. 94), Corinne Tye (p.
97), iStock/Diane Diederich (p. 3, 108), National Library of Canada (p. 114: C-59399),
National Archives of Canada (p. 121: C-1833; p. 214: PA-111125; p. 224: C-10212), Nova
Scotia Museum (p. 127: B-08392), Nova Scotia Archives (p. 105, 133), Heritage
Foundation of Newfoundland and Labrador (p. 4-5, 143, 145, 151, 154), Provincial
Archives of Newfoundland and Labrador (p. 158), O'Keefe Ranch (p. 161, 170, 172),
iStock/Jeffrey McDonald (p. 180), Willow Place Inn (p. 207), Corel (p. 203, 210, 212),
Bibliothéque Nationale de Québec (p. 220), Edouard Gauvin (p. 233).

We acknowledge the financial support of the Government of Canada through the Book
Publishing Industry Development Program (BPIDP) for our publishing activities.

PC: P6

To Grampa Murray, KB,
Leida Finlayson and those who believe

Contents

Acknowledgements 6

Introduction 8

Chapter One: Ontario

Bytown Museum OTTAWA, ON 11

Château Laurier OTTAWA, ON 17

Harbourfront-du Maurier Theatre TORONTO, ON 19

Fright in Fort Frances FORT FRANCES, ON 24

Merritt House ST. CATHARINES, ON 29

Obies Restaurant TORONTO, ON 34

Pickering Poltergeist PICKERING, ON 37

Spook Lights at Buck Hill OTTAWA VALLEY, ON 39

Texas Road AMHERSTBURG, ON 41

Haunted Steamer LAKE SUPERIOR 44

The Former Lakeshore Psychiatric Hospital TORONTO, ON 48

The Guild Inn SCARBOROUGH, ON 52

The Homeless Ghost HAMILTON, ON 58

The Rattling Door COLDWATER, ON 60

The Tunnel Creature TORONTO, ON 64

Chapter Two: The Prairies

Who's Scared Now? WINNIPEG, MB 68

A Partridge, a Pear Tree and a Ghost WINNIPEG, MB 74

Not Your Average Childhood SHILO, MB 80

St. Louis Lights ST. LOUIS, SK 86

A Strange and Gifted Life WINNIPEG, MB 93

Chapter Three: The Maritimes

Grandma's Rocking Chair FREDERICTON, NB 106

The Club Has a Ghostly Member HALIFAX, NS 111

He Hears Dead People DEADMAN'S ISLAND, NS 113

The Five Fishermen and a Few Ghosts HALIFAX, NS 120

The Headless Ghost of the Isle of Haute BERWICK, NS 126

The Legend of Double Alex SAMBRO ISLAND, NS 131
The Burning Ship BAIE DES CHALEURS, NB 138

Chapter Four: Newfoundland

Strange Happenings at the Long Point Light TWILLINGATE, NL 144
The One That Got Away ARGENTIA, NL 147
The Jib-boom Ghost ST. JOHN'S, NL 150
The Harbour Grace Corpse Light HARBOUR GRACE, NL 153
The Ghost of Graveyard Cove EMILY HARBOUR, NL 156

Chapter Five: British Columbia

Music in the Walls AGASSIZ, BC 162
Brady and His Lady—Ghosts at the Bedford Regency VICTORIA, BC 164
O'Keefe Ranch VERNON, BC 169
Phantom of the Burn Unit VANCOUVER, BC 174
Sabrina's Surrey Spectre SURREY, BC 175
The Alibi Room VANCOUVER, BC 179
The Falling Phantom VANCOUVER, BC 182
Emily's Ghost at the James Bay Inn VICTORIA, BC 185
The Man-Loving Ghost ABBOTSFORD, BC 191
The Thetis Lake Monster VICTORIA, BC 194
The Townhouse Spectres VANCOUVER, BC 196

Chapter Six: Québec

King George Park WESTMOUNT, QC 204
Maud of the Willow Place Inn HUDSON, QC 205
Montréal's Ghosts MONTRÉAL, QC 209
The Centaur Theatre MONTRÉAL, QC 215
The Ghost of Mary Gallagher MONTRÉAL, QC 219
The Ghost of the Cathedral QUÉBEC CITY, QC 223
The Hudson Poltergeist HUDSON, QC 228
The Old Ramsay Chapel MAGOG, QC 230
The Memphrémagog Monster NEAR MAGOG, QC 231
Champie, the Monster of Lake Champlain LAKE CHAMPLAIN 236

Acknowledgements

Many thanks to Laurie Thatcher of Ghost Tours of Quebec, Graham Conway of UFOBC, Heather Anderson of BC's Ghosts and Hauntings Research Society (GHRS), Matthew Didier of Ontario's GHRS, Sue Darroch of Para-Researchers of Ontario and Kyle Archibald, Ken Sooley, Ian Harper and Glen Shackleton of the Haunted Walk of Ottawa. —*Susan Smitten*

Most of the stories about the Prairies came to me through the generosity of Carolin Vesely at the *Winnipeg Free Press*, who wrote about my hunt for accounts. Thank you, Carolin. Jean, Kelly, Cory, your candor was refreshing. Thank you to Will Chabun of the *Regina Leader-Post* and to Linda Horodecki of the Manitoba Legislative Library. Others shared their stories with me, but while I cannot mention their names, I do want to tell them how much I appreciate being able to write about their experiences. Bruce Howie, I'll get around to your story someday. And finally, thank you to Ghost House Books, notably the self-proclaimed Apex of Fun, Dan Asfar, and Nancy Foulds and Shane Kennedy. And to Kristi Borrmann—for the smiles and the laughter—I owe you. —*Edrick Thay*

Researching and writing any book or portion of a book requires the support and assistance of many people. The stories in this collection from the Maritime region would not have been possible without the generosity and assistance of the following people: Joan Balcom, Miguel Romero, Jason Clarke, Leonard Currie, Drew Curlett, Chris Mills, Carol Livingston, Darryll Walsh and Audrey Doane. These people have my undying gratitude for their willingness to share their stories and knowledge of the supernatural. As well, I must express my sincere thanks to the people of Ghost House Books, particularly Nancy Foulds and Chris Wrangler. As in the past, they have made this project an enjoyable experience. A special note of thanks to researcher Chris Mills and the Nova Scotia Lighthouse Preservation Society for the use of this material. —*Vernon Oickle*

If ever there was a group of people who love telling and listening to ghost stories, it is the people of Newfoundland and Labrador. Many thanks to all those who have shared their tales with me over the years. In particular, very special thank yous to George Jones, Kelly Jones, Leander Martin, Jack May, Louise Vallis and the staff of the Centre for Newfoundland Studies. I also owe a great deal of thanks to all those people who have taken part in the St. John's Haunted Hike walking tour since 1997—Newfoundlanders, Labradorians and Come-From-Aways alike—and to Mark Scott, Gabe Newman, Steve O'Connell and David Walsh, my fellow ghoulish guides. —*Dale Jarvis*

Introduction

No matter where you live in Canada, whether on the rocky bluffs of Newfoundland or under the cherry blossoms of Victoria, there is at least one common aspect to our folklore—every area has its ghosts. After hundreds of interviews with people across the country, it seems that it's a rare house that hasn't been visited by spirits—at least once.

Releasing the need to control reality is difficult, even for the living, and departed souls seem to take their own time letting go. Spirits work in a different rhythm, returning many years after death to work, visit loved ones or tend to unfinished business. Those that return to complete a task or to bring something hidden to light seem to hang around much longer, often for centuries. They are also much more active and more easily discerned. Such souls are not generally known to harm the living, although they might scare them to get their attention or to make a point. Many obsessed spirits seem so immersed in a personal quandary that they are completely oblivious to the living. The living, however, are acutely aware of the spirits.

Ghost stories exist everywhere, in all cultures and throughout history. People love to ponder the mystery of whether souls remain tethered to this earthly plane. Many believe outright that this is fact. Others remain skeptical, preferring to adopt an I'll-believe-it-when-I-see-it attitude.

This book chronicles the experiences of ordinary Canadians who rarely sought ghosts deliberately but somehow found them just the same. The people in the following pages met ghosts, sometimes up close and personal, sometimes at a distance, causing them to doubt their own judgment. They heard them, smelled them, saw them, spoke to them and, in rare cases, helped them. Some took photographs and made audio recordings to lend credence to their tales. For many of these people, there is no question that ghosts do indeed exist and haunt us. Some still wonder if what they experienced wasn't just a wicked case of mental gas. We present these stories as told to us so that readers may decide for themselves.

The stories are as varied as the Canadian landscape. This collection was a team effort: Dale Jarvis collected stories from Newfoundland, Vernon Oickle covered the Maritimes, Edrick Thay wrote those from the Prairies and Susan Smitten contributed accounts from Québec, Ontario and British Columbia. Some witnesses prefer to remain anonymous, so their names have been changed, and addresses have been left vague to protect their privacy. The rest include actual names and locations. Some stories are well known in their respective communities, such as those of Ottawa's Bytown Museum or Victoria's Bedford Regency Hotel. Most, however, receive their first public notoriety in this book. They run the gamut from amusing to tragic to deeply disturbing, but what they do share in common is that they all happened to average Canadians who were kind enough to share their experiences.

1
Ontario

Bytown Museum
OTTAWA, ON

The sound of heavy, booted footsteps is the trademark of the ghost at Bytown Museum in Ottawa. Fellow ghost story chronicler Barbara Smith touched on the ghostly goings-on in her first book of *Ontario Ghost Stories*. Since then, there have been several strange incidents, including a few that might shed light on who the mysterious presence could be.

The museum is the oldest stone building in Ottawa. Built in 1827, it originally housed military supplies and money needed for the construction of the Rideau Canal from Ottawa to Kingston. Now it holds the history of both the canal's construction and early life in old Bytown, Ottawa's original name.

Glen Shackleton believes Bytown Museum is *the* most haunted building in the city. As the operator of the Haunted Walk of Ottawa, he should know. But even more to the point, he witnessed a paralyzing display of the paranormal first-hand while in the old stone structure.

"It's ironic," says Shackleton wryly. "I'm a huge chicken, and you can quote me on that!"

In October 2000, employees for Shackleton's tour company had planned to go to the museum for their staff party. Glen is also the chair for the volunteer board that manages the museum, so he had access to the facility. He and a few others arrived early, and while they waited for the rest of the group, some of the tour guides showed their skeptical side and urged the ghost to show itself.

The identity of the ghost at Ottawa's Bytown Museum remains a mystery.

One of the guides, according to Shackleton, did his best to antagonize the spirit that resides there, calling out, "Hey Duncan! Show yourself!"

The popular belief is that the ghost could be that of Duncan MacNab, one of the first storekeepers who ran the supply shop. MacNab had a reputation as a bit of a trickster. Rum and other supplies often disappeared while under his care. One time, when a large amount of rum vanished, MacNab reported that it had "evaporated." Records also show that a week's rations were given out to a man who had died, although MacNab had no explanation for where the rations had gone. Given his reputation as a dissembler and thus the type to haunt a museum, he was the man the group taunted to appear. Nothing happened, and in the end the group changed the party location to a nearby pub. But the heckling may have set the stage for what occurred a few hours later.

At around 11:30 PM, Shackleton realized that he had forgotten to reset the alarms in the museum. Not wanting to return alone, he asked a few volunteers to go with him.

"I'm not the kind of person to spend a night in a haunted house," admits Glen. Two of his tour guides, Emily and Margo, and Emily's mother, who was in town visiting, agreed to accompany him.

Inside the deserted museum, they decided to show Emily's mother some of the more interesting exhibits on the third floor, such as the plaster cast of famous murder victim D'Arcy McGee. Glen says that the first sign of something unusual came as he and Margo headed downstairs. On the staircase at the second floor, the loud and distinct sound of footsteps seemed to move up the stairs towards Glen.

"I could see no one but heard the 'thump, thump, thump.' I knew that the front door was locked so no one else could get in."

Margo confirmed that she heard the sound, too. Thinking it could be the others walking about, they called up, but the two hadn't moved.

They returned to the first floor of the museum, which houses the museum gift shop and Parks Canada offices. Ready to leave, Shackleton gathered everyone by the front door. In order to set the motion detectors, they had to be still, and the doors had to be closed. He shut the heavy door to the Parks Canada area and was about to set the alarm code, when the door began to shake. It vibrated gently at first, as if a truck was passing outside.

"But remember, this is a stone building built to withstand a cannon attack," notes Shackleton. "It doesn't shake." Within seconds, the door began to shake violently. "Like it was coming off its hinges, as if someone on the other side was beating it again and again." Looking in the security camera monitor, he could see that no one was on the other side of the door.

"By this time, I am absolutely paralyzed with fear," says Shackleton. "I don't do fight or flight. I just stand there frozen." To make matters worse, his support group raced out of the building, leaving him there alone. "I called out, 'Don't leave me here!' and Margo came back."

Outside, Glen debriefed with the others. "I said, 'Can you believe that?' and to my amazement no one knew what I was talking about. They didn't see the door shake. Instead, the three all heard heavy boots coming in their direction across the floor above them. That was why they all ran." Shackleton had not heard the footsteps, and they hadn't seen the door shake.

Later, when he interviewed each person individually, their description of what they heard matched exactly. "I have since tried to recreate that shaking, but I couldn't do it," says the tour operator. No one else was in the building at the time, and he has yet to explain what happened.

Since then, numerous strange things have occurred to convince Glen that the museum is truly haunted. One Halloween, he went up to get D'Arcy McGee's hand to display downstairs and found the locked cabinet door wide open.

"I had the only key with me. It was bizarre."

Lights turn off or on with no explanation. On one occasion, the staff shut down all breakers and still had one set of lights that would not go off. A director of the museum heard the voices of two men arguing. Many people hear the heavy tread of someone wearing boots walking across the floor. And employees frequently hear someone whistling in the building in areas where no one is present.

An interpreter who worked in the building for five years felt she was constantly the brunt of some phantom prank. Solid plastic covers on the third floor ceiling's sprinkler system would routinely pop off, although they normally required tools to be removed. Historical videos and films would turn on and off when no one was in the room.

Another incident involved one of the museum displays, which is the recreation of a card game in progress. There is a table with playing cards laid out as though in mid-game. One of the staff members told the museum director that when she arrived each day, the cards would be placed in a different pattern. Since she closed up at night and was the first one to return in the morning, she found the reshuffling somewhat disturbing. She swore it happened several times, so one night she and the director arranged the cards in a particular way and then they left together, setting the alarm and locking up. The next day, they came in together and, to their astonishment, found all the cards on the floor in a heap. No windows were open, and this had never happened before. Everyone agreed it was strange and could find no explanation for how it might have happened.

When Shackleton first investigated the museum's history, he felt sure the ghost was that of Duncan MacNab because of his track record as a prankster. Subsequently, he has had other experiences that suggest he might have been wrong.

"One of the gift shop employees told me she's convinced the ghost has it in for me because we name the wrong person in our tours. He's trying to get our attention."

The woman pointed out that whenever Shackleton talked about MacNab, something electrical would go wrong. To emphasize the point, during a conversation with the employee, Glen asked if she had heard from Duncan MacNab. At that moment, her computer shut down by itself and rebooted. On the blue screen the name "Colonel John By" appeared over and over. She could find nothing in the computer to make it do such a thing. Colonel By built the entire Rideau Canal system, and he had the museum building constructed as a storage facility. He would have spent time there, but he certainly didn't live in the building.

"I'm not sure what to make of it. It was a creepy way to get my attention," says Shackleton.

Could the voices of the two angry men be MacNab and the colonel, duking it out over some bygone supply indiscretion? Or are they having an otherworldly spat over who gets the credit for the current unexplainable events at the museum?

Château Laurier
OTTAWA, ON

Regal and elegant, the Château Laurier hotel is the centre-piece of Canada's capital city. It rests majestically between Parliament Hill, the Ottawa River, the Congress Centre and the open-air Byward Market. Hotel guests step back in time, surrounded by cathedral ceilings, brass stair rails, marble floors and antiques. And while the Château enchants visitors with its stateliness, it may also enthrall them with its supernatural entities.

In 1907, American-born entrepreneur Charles Melville Hays commissioned the hotel. Hays was general manager of the Grand Trunk Pacific Railway, and he saw the Château Laurier as the railway's flagship hotel. To reflect the elegance and grandeur of the times, the hotel was built to resemble a French castle. Ross and Macfarlane Contractors built the hotel in a French Renaissance style using granite blocks for the base, buff Indiana limestone for the walls and copper for the roof. Hays wanted the social elite of the time to come to his palace, waltz in the ballroom and smoke cigars while quaffing port in the reading room.

During construction of the impressive structure, Charles Hays could often be heard whistling on site as he watched his dream take shape. Several weeks before the historic grand opening, Hays sailed to London, England, to purchase furnishings for the dining room. After making his purchases he decided on another momentous first, and bought a first-class ticket back to Canada on board the RMS *Titanic*.

Although Charles Hays perished on the Titanic, *many believe his spirit haunts the lavish Château Laurier.*

On April 14, 1912, Hays and most of the male members of his party perished in the cold Atlantic. Only Paul Chevre, who sculpted the bust of Prime Minister Wilfrid Laurier, and the women in Hays' party, including his wife, Clara, survived the disaster. Charles Hays never saw the opening of his splendid hotel two months later. Or did he?

Many believe that Mr. Hays' attachment to his hotel drew his spirit back to its halls. Visitors claim to hear soft whistling in different parts of the hotel, only to discover that no one is there. Others report seeing a mysterious man in a dark cloak on the fifth floor, a man who then disappears without a trace. Some fifth-floor guests have spotted an old man dressed in period clothes, while others have felt a hand come to rest on their shoulders when alone in their hotel rooms. A wraith-like figure once accosted well-known CBC personality Patrick Watson on a stairwell, and on another occasion, a woman fled in panic when things began moving around her room of their own accord.

Who is the man roaming the fifth-floor corridors? Employees at the hotel, now part of the Fairmont chain, are reluctant to talk about their resident ghost. But since the flesh-and-blood Charles Melville Hays missed seeing his hotel's unveiling, many believe he remains spiritually shackled to his dream. The consensus is that he is watching to ensure his pride and joy continues to be maintained at a level that suits his standards.

Harbourfront-du Maurier Theatre
TORONTO, ON

"It's a very strange environment." That's Ian Harper's take on Harbourfront Centre in Toronto. He should know; he's worked there for 15 years, and in that time he has both seen and heard the phantoms that live in the theatre. "These are ghosts, as in disembodied entities, not just residual spirit energy. They seem to want to communicate."

Harper works as a sound engineer in the du Maurier Theatre, one of many theatre venues in the complex, which also houses the Premier Dance Theatre and York Quay Centre. The historic structure and its sister building, the Power Plant, were built side-by-side near the Lake Ontario waterfront in 1926 as part of Queen's Quay Terminal. Ships would bring cargo that was stored in these buildings, which had railway lines running to them. The du Maurier Theatre originally served as a giant icehouse where ice cut from the lake in winter was used to preserve perishables being stored before transport.

The former industrial building underwent a massive transformation in 1992 and emerged as a theatre arts centre. At least three ghosts have made their debut since the doors opened for business. The trio of entities includes a mid-30s man, a woman and a child who plays an eternal game of hide-and-seek.

Ian Harper's first encounter with the ghosts occurred a few years ago during "World Stage." The theatre hosts companies from all over the globe for the three-week event. Harper worked in the du Maurier setting up one of the shows.

"We were in the middle of setting it up, and about two dozen people were present in the room—actors and technicians," he recalls. The room was dark except for the lights hitting the stage. He ran up the stairs to the lighting and sound control room when he suddenly realized that a man blocked his way. "I looked up just as I was about to collide with someone standing on the stairs. Instead, I ran right through him."

When he passed through the ghost, Harper experienced a sudden sense of vertigo and lost his balance. "One of the crew asked if I was okay, and I said, 'Oh, I just tripped,' because I didn't know about the ghosts at that point and didn't know what to say."

Later that same week, Harper had his second experience. During a sold-out performance of a show, he was working at a sound console at the back of the theatre rather than in the sound booth. The set-up was beside an exit door.

"At one point in the show, an actor [was to come] through the door and [give] me a large sweater and sweat pants to be used by an actress later in the show." But while Harper stood at the console, out of the corner of his eye he saw a man standing near him. Thinking it was the actor, Harper turned to ask why he was there so early. "The man did not acknowledge my presence. He just vanished before my eyes."

A couple of years ago he met another of the ghosts. On his way from the storage area to the stage while setting up for a corporate rental, Harper saw a small child crouched behind the stage door. He turned to ask the little boy what he was doing, and the boy vanished before his eyes.

"He made eye contact with me. I can still vividly see the look on his face, like 'Oh, you caught me!' in his game of hide-and-seek," says Ian. "Then it was like turning a TV off. The image just dissipated."

Other employees in the du Maurier have also encountered the three ghosts. Many of the cleaning staff are so terrified that where some won't go into the space alone when it's dark. A security guard making night rounds was surprised to walk into the theatre at 4 AM and find a woman sitting in the middle of the venue. The guard naturally went over to ask her what she was doing there. She said to him, "What time does the next show start?" Having uttered her question, she didn't wait for a response but disappeared before the startled man's eyes. He quit the next day.

Harper has not yet met the female ghost but he did have another unnerving sighting of the male entity. He was again at the back of the theatre, this time doing the sound mix for a live Cajun band. The house was half empty because of bad weather.

"Looking around in the balcony area, I saw someone that looked like he was about to fall. I could see a man making an odd arm gesture." Harper's attention returned to his work, and when he looked back, he could still make out a shadow or someone moving in the balcony. He asked others through his headset if they could see it, but no one else had a view of that area of the theatre. Harper couldn't shake the image of the arm gesture over the side of the balcony.

In November 2001, Para-Researchers of Ontario investigated the du Maurier Theatre after hearing stories from Ian and other employees. Two sensitives joined the group to add their impressions to the mix.

Inside the theatre, one of the women said to Harper, "Ian, have you ever seen this before?" The woman made the same arm gesture that the man in the balcony had made. Shocked, he told the woman he had. "He's showing you something," she explained. "He likes you. He knows you care about him. He's showing you how he died. He's reaching for a rope or chain, and he's falling."

The news disturbed Ian. "Normally, this stuff doesn't bug me. I've lived in a haunted house. But this creeped me out."

While in the building, the investigators and theatre staff simultaneously witnessed an "amber ball of light" pass by while they stood in the stage area. The two women with paranormal sensitivity picked up on impressions of a male entity with a sense of humour.

On December 2, 2001, another group of paranormal investigators and researchers visited the du Maurier to search for the entities there. In addition to sensing centres of paranormal energy, one of the group also caught sight of something strange.

While talking with Ian Harper near the stage, Matthew Didier of Toronto's Ghosts and Hauntings Research Society reported that he saw what he thought was one of the other researchers "bolt out of sight" through a doorway up on the theatre's third level.

"One problem," notes Didier. "Steve was very visible and on the stage at the time." Didier was surprised that what he saw appeared quite solid, not the traditional diaphanous image of a ghost.

Initially, the researchers could not find any connection between the ghosts and the building's history. In a building mainly used as a warehouse, it seemed especially odd that the ghosts actually used the theatre and were aware of its layout and architecture. Often, ghosts haunt places as they looked at the time of their deaths, thus defying logic by walking through walls and floating. With research, one usually finds that the original floor plans show a doorway or other exit, and floaters are walking on a floor or in a stairwell that has been removed. As well, there didn't seem to be any record of people dying in the building.

But when Ian Harper looked into the history a little further, he uncovered some details that might account for the ghosts. "A ship had caught fire in the Toronto harbour, and a lot of people were killed. In historical references, it is clear that emergency workers used an icehouse in the harbour as a temporary morgue."

Recently, Harper related the following incident. "I just finished doing a bunch of work in the du Maurier Theatre. A lighting technician and good friend of mine, who had been filling in for the house tech, told me that he had been walking down the back hall when he saw a woman bent over, as if looking for something. At first he thought it was another tech that we work with, but she was not on the crew call. When he called out to her, she went all shadowy and disappeared. I've known this fellow for a few years, and he is pretty level-headed so he was quite surprised at what he saw. While I was there, I saw the male spirit moving around the balconies a few times. But here's a first for me. I was pushed or shoved while I was working alone up in one of the balconies, and I could hear from time to time what I could only call whispering."

With all of these incidents on record, it seems that the du Maurier Theatre is certainly haunted and a very strange place indeed.

Fright in Fort Frances

FORT FRANCES, ON

Imagination is a powerful force and rarely more so than in the mind of a child. Unfettered by boundaries—either real or imposed—children create entire worlds and often populate them with people they like. But what if an imaginary friend is not of the child's making, but rather a nasty spirit that begins to terrorize with threats of violence? Such was the case with one Ontario family. Their story is truly chilling. At their request, we have changed their names to protect their privacy.

"Joan" and "Don" moved to Fort Frances in the early 1980s. The first year or more in their new home gave no indication of the terror they were about to experience.

"Things were fine and normal," says Joan.

Then Joan began to notice flashes of light in a particular area of the kitchen. The light caught her attention because it usually happened in the early evening or after dark, when she wasn't in the room and the lights were off. Whenever the flashes occurred, Joan checked to see if something had caused a reflection. The room had two windows, one over the sink and one to the left of it, and Joan thought perhaps the flashes originated outside. But every time she looked, she realized again that her neighbour's house blocked anything that would shine through. No reflection could come in from either of the two windows, and nothing else in the kitchen or nearby rooms seemed to cause the light flashes. The flashes happened infrequently so were not alarming—at first.

Then the paranormal activity escalated. Joan began hearing someone or something softly saying her name. "It would not quite whisper, not quite speak my name," she recalls. "More like a loud whisper. Each time it caught me off guard and even though I *knew* no one was in the house, I would look for someone anyway." At first, Joan thought their basement suite tenant was playing tricks on her, but she ruled that out. "I know what I heard, and no one was there."

One particularly creepy event took place when Joan was pregnant with their second child and when her youngest daughter, "Anne," was three. It happened on a day when Don was working a late shift that finished at midnight. Joan had already put Anne to bed.

"My husband had a routine when he came home. If late, he would quietly click the kitchen door shut, and I would hear his feet on the mat at the back door. Then I would hear the sliding closet door bearings click when he opened it to put away his jacket. This night, *both* my daughter and I heard the back door open."

"Daddy's home!" Anne shouted. Joan told her excited toddler to stay in bed, and she would send Don in to kiss her good night.

Joan had been watching television, and she waited on the sofa for her husband's arrival. Then she realized she couldn't hear any other sounds. She knew the tenant in the basement was away for the weekend, so she assumed her husband had had a stressful day at work and would join her when he was ready. Her daughter fell asleep waiting for Don, who did not appear.

"Finally I realized that something was not right, and I was concerned that something was wrong with my husband," says Joan.

She checked throughout the house to see where he had gone; Don was nowhere to be found. She double-checked that her tenant had not returned early, but his suite was empty. Finally, Joan looked outside where it had been snowing. No tire tracks led to the garage.

"Now, I *knew* I'd heard the back door close because my daughter heard it too. But I also heard the shuffling of his feet on the mat and the closet door," emphasizes Joan. Some time later, Don did come home. It was then that Joan looked at the clock and noted he was on time. "It hadn't occurred to me to look at the clock before." When Joan asked her husband if, by chance, he had dropped by the house earlier that evening, he said no. And he did not take the news of a back-door phantom very well. "He was not impressed with the previous 'happenings,' and it was starting to scare him."

Around the same time, Anne occasionally mentioned the "white man." At first, Joan assumed this was a standard, child-created, invisible playmate. After hearing about the "white man" a few times, Joan finally asked for more details. Anne revealed that her "friend" told her things.

"But these were not things that a child of three dreams up," Joan points out. "He would advise her of certain details of my childhood, and how she should not play in the street because we had a train depot down the street from our home."

Joan's father was murdered when she was a young child, but she remembered that his hair had turned prematurely white by age 18. She started to wonder if her father's ghost might be the "white man." That would also help to explain the voice that called her by name. However, Anne told her mother that the "white man" had stopped coming right after Joan pressed her daughter for details. Still, the whispers and light flashes continued. Joan didn't pay much attention until Anne started talking about her new invisible friend, "Jenny."

At first, Jenny seemed to fit the imaginary friend scenario until "things started to get scary." Anne was terrified of Jenny and expressed concern that she would hurt the new baby when it arrived. Joan put the talk down to toddler jealousy but soon realized her three-year-old was frightened by Jenny. Then came the threats of violence. Jenny threatened to hurt the parents first, then the new baby.

"One time, Anne came into the kitchen shaking, saying that Jenny had said she was going to stab the new baby with a big knife," Joan remembers. "Anne was terrified and crying so hard that it was all I could do to console her."

Then things started moving around in the house when the family was out. When they came home, everything would be subtly shifted. Dishes in the china hutch were in a different order or a picture hung upside down.

As the poltergeist activity persisted, the family decided to move into a larger home. Jenny told a distraught Anne that she intended to move with them, upsetting the little girl so much that Joan snapped and told Jenny out loud she was not welcome in the new home. The warning had little effect, since Jenny appeared two months later in the new house.

At her wit's end, Joan told Jenny that her hold over the family must come to an end. "I said that a priest would be there the next week, and that she no longer had control over Anne." Jenny apparently took Joan at her word. The terrifying spirit left and did not return.

To this day, Joan is not sure how they attracted such a horrible, mean-spirited entity. She has consulted many experts and friends about imaginary playmates and the response of a child to a new baby, "but I have never heard of a child deathly afraid of an imaginary friend."

Could it be that the nasty spirit accidentally stumbled across Anne through the visits by her grandfather's ghost? Or maybe Anne's initial jealousies over a new sibling roused the sleeping spirit in the house, who then used that energy to execute its reign of terror? In any case, it caused Joan to take her daughter's invisible friends a little more seriously, especially when those friends are not just interested in tea parties and harmless games.

Merritt House
ST. CATHARINES, ON

The house at 12 Yates Street in St. Catharines ranks as one of the most haunted properties in Canada. At least that is the opinion of many Ontario paranormal research groups.

"That place blows my mind," Tamara Zyganiuk of Canadian Scientific Paranormal Investigations told the *Toronto Star* in 1999. "If they wanted us to spend an entire weekend there, I don't think our stress levels would be equipped to handle it rationally. You just never know what is going to happen there."

Merritt House, as it is known, originally belonged to merchant and military man William Hamilton Merritt. Among his many accomplishments, Merritt created the Welland Canal and is considered a hero for his contribution to success in the War of 1812. Merritt's first home on the site, built in the 1820s, burned in a terrible fire in 1858. He then rebuilt the grander, more opulent mansion that stands today. The Merritts didn't enjoy their new home for long because William died only two years after moving into his newly finished house. The house then passed to Jededhiah Prendergast Merritt, William's eldest son.

Since the 19th century, the house has served as an inn, a military convalescent home, a rooming house and finally a radio station. A web of underground tunnels are said to have been part of the Underground Railroad network, and it is believed that they were used by bootleggers as a storage area for contraband whisky shipped south of the border during Prohibition. This varied and rich past has fuelled speculation that the sprawling mansion is home to an equally diverse family of ghosts.

In the late 1990s, radio station CKTB broadcast its talk radio programs from Merritt House. Coincidentally, one of the shows that aired was *The X-Zone*, hosted by Rob McConnell. As the title implies, the show delved into all branches of the paranormal.

One night, during an *X-Zone* broadcast, seemingly inexplicable events began to unfold. "Things happen in Merritt House that defy explanation," mused McConnell to the *Star* reporter. He also classifies himself as a skeptic, estimating that 98.5 per cent of paranormal events ultimately have a more prosaic explanation.

Apparently Jennifer, one of McConnell's producers, announced that if the house really was haunted, then she would like to see a ghost. On cue, the paranormal parade began. First, Jennifer saw the apparition of a man that vanished before her eyes. The same night the phones acted up, and odd sounds were heard over the air. Although no one could hear them in the studio, the sounds of a man laughing, a bell and a sighing woman were clearly audible. The strange goings-on prompted McConnell to contact a team of ghost investigators, led by Matthew Didier of Toronto's Ghosts and Hauntings Research Society and CSPI's Tamara Zyganiuk.

In July 1999, armed with tape recorders, cameras and notepads, the group of six arrived for a night that would exceed all their expectations. In just four hours, the investigators saw doors open and close and objects move of their own accord. They also heard strange sounds and had the sensation of being blocked from entering certain rooms.

Touring the premises, the group climbed the staircase to the attic. Didier suddenly had trouble breathing and felt as if he was having "panic attacks." Later, he described the feeling as "being hit in the chest with a heavy foam bat." Some others in the group also had trouble breathing. An accompanying psychic told them she felt as if someone had died of a heart attack in the home. She also said that she encountered the entity of the lady of the house who felt that the upstairs area was private and should not be open to the public.

In the boardroom at the top of the stairs, which was previously the master bedroom, there have been reports of hearing a crying baby. The investigators found the energy that had caused the breathing problems was even more powerful at the doorway to the boardroom and actually kept them from entering. Didier dashed through the door despite feeling unwelcome, and once inside the room, he heard an ominous creaking. He and the others watched the door slowly closing behind him. He took that as his cue to exit the room quickly. Although others had gone in and out of the room many times, they noted that this was the only time the door had moved.

In the radio station's master control room, a man named Patrick, invited by McConnell to act as a skeptical eyewitness, found his ability to remain neutral sorely tested. Patrick noticed a loving cup trophy sitting at the edge of a bookshelf, so he pushed it to the back of the shelf. Moments later, he saw that the trophy was back at the edge of the shelf. He moved it back again but this time kept an eye on it. Nothing happened. He forgot about it, assuming it was just his imagination, but when he looked back, the trophy was *again* at the edge of the bookshelf. This time he spoke up, telling the group what had happened. He moved it back, and everyone watched. Again, nothing. (You know where this is going.) The minute the group lost interest and stopped watching, the cup changed position.

Jennifer spoke up. "It moved again."

They tested the shelf with a pencil to see if some tremor might account for the movement, but the pencil did not move.

In yet another room, a tape recorder was used to monitor all activity. Most of that tape contains hours of ambient white noise, but towards the end of the night, Zyganiuk says the recorder picked up a high-pitched, mysterious voice saying, "You'll be fine…" The tape was analyzed using a computer program at CKTB, but the voice remains a mystery.

On August 22, 1999, the investigators returned to Merritt House. Although the house felt "more quiet," they still encountered enough to let them know that the spirits knew they were there.

When Zyganiuk entered the boardroom that night, she felt a small shock, like static electricity, zap her ears.

"You literally feel the current running through you," she explains. "I just about jumped out of my skin when it happened."

Upon entering the room, Derek, another volunteer researcher, stopped dead in his tracks. He slowly backed out of the room and told the others that he felt as if someone had "punched him in his chest." Derek later told Matthew Didier, "I'd like to emphasize how strong of a punch I felt in the boardroom. I had indeed felt spooky feelings at the top of the stairs, but nothing nearly as strong as in the boardroom."

Other mysterious happenings elsewhere in the house included cold spots, a flying two-by-four plank and a disembodied child's voice crying, "Mama, Mama." Other station employees claimed to have seen partial apparitions, heard strange sounds and felt the presence of others.

Who could the spirits be? A maid in the home fell down the stairs and died, so she could be causing the phenomena. Psychics visiting the home claim to have contacted Mrs. Merritt, who complained of her husband's bad temper and a "Jeb" or "Jed"—likely the son—who died after drinking bad moonshine.

In September 2001, another group of ghost investigators visited the house and radio station, which had changed to 97.7 HTZ FM, bringing with them psychics Michele Stableford and Kate Kingston. The pair picked up a lot of negative energy. They also encountered several spirits—a little boy, an angry biker and a sad woman whose name begins with "J." Interestingly, in the boardroom, Michele and Kate sensed an old man smoking a pipe; the man had died of a heart attack. This supports the other psychic's reading of the energy and reports of the smell of tobacco in the room. The group also experienced the same sense of being blocked at the top of the stairs to the attic, where the maid's quarters had been.

Merritt House has an incomparable list of paranormal occurrences, and the energy there seems to magnify rather than diminish with time. It certainly remains at the top of Ontario ghost researchers' "Most Haunted" list.

Obies Restaurant
TORONTO, ON

Disembodied voices, apparitions and flying objects made life for the staff at Obies Restaurant in Toronto an almost daily journey into the paranormal. One former employee, who prefers anonymity so we'll call him "David," says his time at the eatery on Islington Avenue from 1993 to 1994 was the strangest of his life.

The street-level restaurant was adjoined to the Journey's End Hotel. During the day, nothing out of the norm seemed to occur, but evenings brought out the ghosts. According to David, many of the staff witnessed the strange happenings. For example, various employees encountered the man with the red hat.

"On many occasions, we would see a man who sat at the corner table in the northwest end of the restaurant," says David. Or did they? Maybe it was a trick of the light, but the man would not be there when someone went to check on him. "Mostly it would be when I would walk by and see someone out of the corner of my eye," says David. "But when I looked back to serve the table, there would be no one there." To leave that particular seat, the person would have to walk right across the restaurant, but no one was ever seen leaving. The one thing all the Obies employees did agree on was a general description of a mid-30s male wearing a red baseball cap.

Objects in the restaurant moved in a most unseemly way, sometimes flying through the air as if tossed by an unseen hand. On one occasion, both staff and customers witnessed a metal coffee filter soar across the room.

"It wasn't that it just fell out or anything like that," recalls David. "It actually flew straight out and landed in the middle of the restaurant—twice." Back in the kitchen, heavy stockpots stored above the dishwasher's area were also known to fly off the shelf. No tremor or shaking could be blamed because the large pots would actually slide sideways down the length of the shelf before launching into the air.

Do ghosts have a sense of humour? Perhaps so. One night, three of the employees became pawns in a weird ghostly gag. David, the cook and the dishwasher were all in different sections of the restaurant. Only a few customers lingered. David recalls that the cook was in his kitchen in the northwest corner; the dishwasher was in the staff area, which is a small alcove at the south end of the building; and David was at the cash register in the northeast section.

"At the same moment, we each heard one of the other's voices call us by name. I heard the cook call me, the dishwasher heard me and the cook heard the dishwasher," says David. "We all met in the middle of the restaurant wondering what the other had wanted. Then we realized none of us had called."

More frightening was the experience of another waiter on staff. He was cleaning up in preparation for closing at around 9 PM and had started refilling and restocking items in the staff area by the coffee station. David recounts the next terrifying moments.

"In the coffee stand was a small cupboard where we kept a garbage pail. When the waiter opened the door to the garbage, bolts of electricity flew at him and literally threw him back. He was distraught by this and screamed as it happened."

Strangely enough, that same night a psychic friend of David's called to say that she had picked up on the activity there and that she sensed a poltergeist in the restaurant.

On another night a friend of David's came to visit with her daughter. As they sat at a table, the lights around her table went out. None of the other restaurant lights were affected. David was stunned because the lights were wired in such a way that they were on two or three different switches, and all the switches were on. Even more astonishing was that when his friend left, all the lights around her table came on again.

David submitted his stories about Obies to Sue Darroch's Para-Researchers of Ontario. Sue says the restaurant and hotel are now closed. There's no way of knowing if the entities that David and others encountered are still there or if they moved on when the business changed hands.

Pickering Poltergeist
PICKERING, ON

For a retired couple in Pickering, hopes for a quiet life in a middle-class suburb have been flipped upside down. After more than 20 years of living peacefully in their four-bedroom home, they now have a ghost. And this particular entity introduced itself somewhat forcefully.

Mr. and Mrs. J (their names are being withheld to protect their privacy) brought up their children in this house. They are well known and well liked in their community. Now that their children are grown, they are alone in their house except for the basement suite, which they have rented to their nephew. He is often away on business.

As far as anyone knows, there is no history of paranormal phenomena at this house, nor is there any record of a tragedy or violent occurrence that might have triggered the ghostly goings-on. Often such accounts provide clues about where the spirit originated. As it stands, Mr. and Mrs. J have no idea who or what is haunting their home. And they certainly don't know why. All they do know is that events have occurred inside their house that they cannot explain.

Among the strange things that have happened are unusual sounds, such as footsteps in parts of the house that are empty. The Js have also encountered cold spots and noticed that various items will disappear and then suddenly reappear. Sometimes covers are pulled off the bed or even rise up while the couple is in bed and wide awake. Mrs. J says that twice she has awakened to discover she is unable to move. That may be attributable to the common sleep disorder known as sleep paralysis, but in light of everything else that is going on in their home, it seems worth adding to the list.

The most distressing event to date happened one night when Mrs. J was in bed reading. She watched her large 4' x 6' dresser mirror lift up, turn on its side and then drop to the floor. Terrified, she screamed for her husband. He found his distraught wife still in bed and the mirror, unbroken, on the floor. Even more peculiar was that nothing else on the dresser had been disturbed. Mrs. J's collection of glass perfume bottles and pictures sat neatly in place. If the mirror had fallen over because of a tremor or a shift in the house, it should have disturbed the items on the dresser or at least should have broken when it fell.

Sue Darroch, an Ontario-based researcher of the paranormal, examined the mirror personally. She found that, although the mirror was not bolted to the wall, it was heavy enough to stay in place on non-skid pads. It had not been moved since it had originally been put in place. She also found that no tremors, not even slight ones, were recorded in the area on the date that the mirror fell.

In her online report, Darroch points to a poltergeist. "This type of phenomenon is usually associated with a teen or young person; however, all occupants of the residence are adults with no apparent emotional issues." The bulk of the poltergeist activity seems to centre on the couple's bedroom, with only a few incidents in other areas of the home.

Understandably, Mr. and Mrs. J find the inexplicable events distressing. Darroch remains in touch with them and says that the couple is too unnerved to discuss the goings-on with anyone else. They simply want whatever is causing the frightening incidents to go away.

Spook Lights at Buck Hill
OTTAWA VALLEY, ON

Parents will agree that no fear matches that of something happening to their children. But could the anguish of parents for a missing child keep them earthbound in an eternal search? In a place called Buck Hill, approximately 90 kilometres from Pembroke in Ontario's Ottawa Valley, there is a ghost story to suggest that it could.

The story takes place during the Depression. As the local lore goes, a particularly vicious winter storm gripped the area. A logger came home to take care of his family, and he warned them to stay indoors while he went out to fetch some firewood. Unfortunately, his warning went unheeded. When he came back with the wood, his wife informed him that one of their pets had somehow run out of the house and their daughter had followed it. The mother was frantic because the girl had not yet returned.

The anxious father grabbed his lantern and went out into the storm in search of his child. He hunted desperately up and down Buck Hill Road but he could not find his little girl. She had vanished into the storm and was never seen again. According to legend, the grieving father descended into madness, refusing to stop searching. He went out with his lantern every night until his death to comb the area for his missing daughter. Some locals say the logger still searches to this day along the isolated road.

The ghost investigators at Para-Researchers of Ontario (PRO) are looking into these stories, and while they haven't found any historical evidence to corroborate the possibility of a ghost in the area, they have found several accounts from witnesses who have seen balls of light along Buck Hill Road. The lights are generally one of three colours: white, amber or green. They are roughly the size of a baseball and have on occasion been bright enough to light up the nearby forest. The spook lights will sometimes flare hotly, becoming larger and more intense before disappearing.

One eyewitness saw the ghost lights on two consecutive nights. On the first occasion, he and two friends watched a green light move slowly down the road, then it suddenly accelerated forward, stopped dead, then reversed in a flash back to its starting point.

The witness said, "It was very spooky. Then as another car came from the valley below, the light wandered off into the bushes." The group waited, and the light returned. "We watched for about 30 seconds as the strange eerie light went from a green to an orange or amber light and then wandered off."

The following night they returned but found a lot of people there partying and playing music. The region is a well-known party spot for teens. The three waited until everyone left and caught a short glimpse of the lights again.

Word of mysterious lights tends to draw crowds, although they may not get the best results. The gang at PRO plans to delve into the anomalies at Buck Hill and has been soliciting reports from witnesses. In the meantime, if you happen to be out on that isolated road one night and catch sight of a lone light meandering along, it may well be the spirit of the grieving logger looking for his lost child.

Texas Road
AMHERSTBURG, ON

Near the southern Ontario town of Amherstburg is the very haunted and decidedly creepy Texas Road. The stories surrounding this remote stretch of pavement involve motorcycle gangs, murderers and a maniacal man with a gun. Is it any wonder that ghosts are said to exist out there?

Local ghost hunter Kyle Archibald says that the isolated stretch of Texas Road that runs between Concession Road 8 and Walker Road seemed to be a hot spot for motorcycle clubs back in the 1970s and 1980s. Although no facts support the rumours, it is said that several gruesome murders occurred in the area.

"I can't validate the stories," Kyle writes, "but I suspect there is some truth mixed in with some legend."

According to Kyle, one ghost is believed to be that of a now-deceased resident of Texas Road who became rather manic after his beloved dogs were killed. The man kept two dogs chained in his front yard, but neighbours complained to the police that the dogs were rabid. Officials arrived at the man's house to destroy the animals and apparently shot them on sight. The distraught owner refused to believe his pets had been diseased, and from that day he held a grudge against his neighbours and the local police. It was said that the man created life-sized effigies of the police officers and could be seen shooting at them from his porch. The man would also sit outside, watching his property to ensure no one else ever set foot on it. He eventually died, but folks around Texas Road say his spirit still roams the property, watching over it for all time.

Travellers brave enough to continue along Texas Road will discover that the road is blocked off, so they must park their cars and travel by foot down to a bridge that crosses a stream. Many urban legends are told about what happened there to fuel imaginations and provide rationale for the existence of ghosts. One common tale is of a man who drowned his two daughters in the stream. Another is that of a man who killed himself by jumping off the bridge into the water. Witnesses report seeing mist-like figures sweeping over the road, and some claim to have seen full apparitions.

A trio of intrepid ghost hunters—Kristy Guitard, Jennifer Holman and Beth Maisonneuve—shared their experiences along Texas Road. The three rely on Kristy's sensitivity to ensure their missions don't lead to danger.

"Kristy is clairvoyant," says Beth, "so we rely on her to let us know if it is safe to go down to Texas Road on any particular night. She has proven to be correct about many things in the past, so we trust that she will be in the future as well."

The girls' first experience shook them. They decided to photograph any paranormal anomalies and went armed with a digital camera. They snapped pictures along the road and up to the place where the road is blocked. Kristy decided to check her digital readout to see what, if anything, she was capturing.

Beth says, "When she looked at the photo on her camera, she was horrified to see a very unpleasant face in a misty haze. The face was distorted into a menacing grin and would have been no more than two feet in front of where we were standing." They saved the image and left immediately, but when they tried to download the image to their computer, it was no longer on the camera.

A few days later, drawn back to try to recapture the image, the team again parked at the bridge and explored the area with their camera. This time they invited three other friends as witnesses. The group noticed sudden cold spots in the area. Kristy and Beth heard what sounded like men talking.

"There were two distinct voices. One man said something to the other, and the second replied," notes Beth. They were not the voices of anyone in their party, and no one else was spotted out there.

Later that same night, the group heard children's voices. Given the late hour, it seemed odd. It was even more unusual when they could not find any children nearby. The photos they took that night seemed to show several orbs and ectoplasm. Beth says it was not be the last time they encountered the auditory phenomenon. "On another occasion, Jennifer heard the sound of children's voices in the style of question and answer."

After their second expedition, Kristy dreamed of a car accident in the mid-1980s in which a young couple died. The dreams prompted the girls to research the area's history, and they found a record of a death that seems to match Kristy's dream. Could the young man and his girlfriend still be haunting the road that claimed their lives?

In addition to all the ghosts along the road, this particular route is also home to "one of the creepiest and most active cemeteries in Essex County," according to Kyle Archibald. On the far side of the bridge, there is a wooded trail that leads to the secluded St. Clement's Cemetery.

"I have witnessed many unexplainable sounds such as crying and a female voice calling out in the distance when no one else was around," says Kyle.

Kyle teamed up with a group of Michigan ghost investigators to explore the cemetery and its phenomena. They have posted digital pictures on their websites of what they believe to be clouds of ectoplasm hovering over some of the grave markers. Kyle writes, "We took some good orb photos at the altar-like memorial. Upon returning to the bridge, we heard something that sounded like a large dog falling out of a tree and hitting the ground hard. Unfortunately we never saw it happen."

While the scenic back roads of southern Ontario are perfect for taking a drive, travellers down Texas Road might get more than they bargained for if they venture down after dark!

Haunted Steamer
LAKE SUPERIOR

The *Emperor* sailed the Great Lakes for 37 years. Its career ended abruptly and in tragedy in 1947 at Isle Royale. The infamous rock caused the *Emperor* to sink, taking 12 men to a cold, watery death. Today, the ship's hull is a favourite haunt of divers—and of ghosts.

Built in 1910 by Collingwood Shipbuilding Co. of Collingwood, Ontario, the *Emperor* initially served as a steel ore steamer for Inland Lines Ltd. before being sold to Canada Steamship Lines. At 525 feet long, with a depth of 27 feet, the

The Emperor *departed from Port Arthur late on the night of June 3, 1947. It sank very early the next morning.*

Emperor was powered by a 1500-horsepower, triple-expansion steam engine that could push the ship at a registered nominal speed of 10 knots.

On June 3, 1947, the *Emperor*'s crew set out with no inkling of the tragedy about to unfold. After loading 10,000 tons of bulk iron ore at the Port Arthur Iron Ore Dock, the *Emperor* departed Port Arthur at 10:55 PM under the command of Captain Eldon Walkinshaw. At midnight, the watch was turned over to First Mate James Morrey. Unfortunately, the exhausted Morrey had spent six gruelling hours loading the vessel. An inquiry later judged that his fatigue probably caused him to skip standard navigational checks as the ship headed towards Passage Island. To compound the problem, the new helmsman was unfamiliar with this part of the lake, so he did not catch the error in the ship's heading. The ship, powered by its mighty engine, plowed straight towards a bank of deadly rocks.

At 4:15 AM on June 4, 1947, the *Emperor* ran hard onto Canoe Rocks. It sank within 30 minutes. Twelve of the crew died, including Captain Walkinshaw and First Mate Morrey. Most of the casualties occurred as the sinking ship sucked a lifeboat down, carrying the frantic crew under.

The U.S. Coast Guard cutter *Kimball* was in the vicinity and luckily reached the site within a half hour of receiving the distress call. She arrived just in time for her crew to pluck the nearly frozen survivors from the icy waters of Lake Superior.

In the half century since she sank, the *Emperor* has drawn dozens of divers to explore the steamer's remains. Their stories cause shivers that have nothing to do with Lake Superior's cold temperature. One diver reported that he swam into a crew cabin to find the apparition of a sailor lying peacefully on his bunk. The ghost looked blankly at the diver, and the astonished diver quickly returned to the surface, having seen enough.

Other divers report hearing the sounds of the ship's engine, despite its rather obvious incapacity. But more frightening is an account of divers hearing voices while exploring the shipwreck. One heard a metallic voice clearly saying "Die!" twice. Another intrepid explorer came upon a ghost that must have been a member of the engine crew.

"The eyes were dark pools of nothing, really just black holes, but they still asked the silent questions, 'Why me? Why am I alone?' " The aqueous apparition went back to his now eternal task of checking the equipment in the engine room, apparently unaware of the layers of dirt and muck sifted onto it by the water's movement.

Some divers, however, chalk all reports up to a deep-sea phenomenon called nitrogen narcosis. Ken Merryman of Superior Trips has run diving trips to the *Emperor* since 1975 and says he hasn't encountered any ghosts.

He says, "I don't recall anyone telling me of seeing anything strange. That doesn't mean it didn't happen, I suppose."

Merryman recalls that in the mid-1970s, divers did find the body of one of the victims. The unfortunate crewman's remains were trapped in the engine room, face down.

"There was nothing paranormal about it—that was a real body," says Merryman.

The dives to the *Emperor* are fairly deep. One dive by the rudder goes to a maximum depth of 165 feet. At the stern, where the engine room and bunkrooms are, it is about 100 feet deep.

Merryman suspects that divers at that depth are suffering from too little oxygen to the brain. He describes the effects of nitrogen narcosis as like having several martinis. "You get visual narrowing, perceptual narrowing as it gets stronger. It also varies a lot with individuals. Reasoning is somewhat impaired."

Merryman is an engineer who runs a hobby diving business during the two months each summer when the water is warm enough and the weather is fair. Many questions remain about the unusual stories. Are they depth-induced hallucinations? Or is something supernatural still lurking in that hulking old wreck?

The Former Lakeshore Psychiatric Hospital
TORONTO, ON

It may seem clichéd that a former insane asylum ranks as one of the "busiest haunts in Toronto." However, this assessment of the former Lakeshore Psychiatric Hospital, made by a paranormal research group, is based on the sheer number of reports of ghostly activity that have come from security guards, students, visitors and construction workers. In the eerie tunnels underneath the buildings, the sound of whistling and the ghost of a former nurse have been heard and seen, much to the chagrin of those travelling the passageways.

The grounds are now home to Humber College's School of Social and Community Services. Set amid 99 acres of parkland, three of the historic renovated cottages of the former hospital house the school's programs. The site, bounded to the south by Lake Ontario, offers students a quiet, reflective environment in which to pursue their studies.

Those same meditative surroundings were first designed with mental health in mind. Built during the 1880s, the former Lakeshore Psychiatric Hospital—originally known as Mimico Hospital for the Insane, or Mimico Asylum—was designed as a village-like complex with shaded walks, beautiful gardens and even a farm. Although most 19th-century asylums conjure up horrible images of suffering and medieval treatments, in reality the original hospital strove to give patients the best possible care for that era.

The prevailing medical opinion at the time held that insanity was an organic brain disease, but that it was most

Do ghosts of dead patients inhabit the former Lakeshore Psychiatric Hospital, now part of Humber College?

often brought on by environmental psychological stresses. It followed that if insanity was the product of a faulty social environment, then it could be cured by placing the insane in a controlled "therapeutic" environment—an asylum. It was for this reason that such lavish attention was devoted to every detail of asylum architecture. Everything about the asylum was geared to be curative.

The Lakeshore Psychiatric Hospital offered the latest treatments to patients until the 1970s, when governments ceased funding residential mental health care. LPH was then used as an outpatient mental health clinic and drug rehabilitation centre until 2001, when Humber College purchased the site and turned many of the buildings into study centres.

Tales of ghosts and rumours of odd incidents began surfacing when the renovations began. A security officer, who asked to remain anonymous, told the Toronto Ghosts and Hauntings Research Society (TGHRS) of a construction worker who'd had a frightening experience in the tunnels. The worker said that he was walking through the dim underground hallway when he rounded a corner and saw a woman walking ahead of him. The woman was oblivious to his presence and even ignored him when he called out to her. She just continued walking and disappeared around a corner. It then dawned on the worker that the woman was wearing a nurse's uniform, but it was much too late for her to be in the tunnel.

Naturally curious, the worker kept following to see where the nurse might be going at such a late hour. When he rounded the corner, he was surprised to see the woman at the far end of the tunnel hallway. She had been out of sight for only a few seconds. She would have had to sprint to reach that distance. The labourer called out again, and this time the woman responded, turning to face him. As she did, he realized the figure was faceless. The terrifying sight sent the man running in the opposite direction, and he refused to ever enter the tunnels again.

Another occurrence in the tunnels took place shortly after the construction had finished. Some students exploring the underground halls heard what they thought was someone whistling behind them. However, they hadn't encountered anyone as they walked through the tunnel and there wasn't anywhere someone could hide. They headed for the stairs to leave, and just as they were about to exit, they heard the whistling again. There was no one in sight, but they reported feeling a cold gust of wind.

Initially, the security guard took these stories and others to be the result of overactive imaginations and the power of suggestion. That is, until he himself worked the midnight shift at the renovated hospital buildings.

On his third night patrolling the grounds, something inside one of the administrative buildings caught his eye. Thinking someone had somehow bypassed the motion sensors, he immediately investigated. The alarm system was still on and armed, so the guard had to turn it off to enter the building. In the darkness, there was a sudden loud noise. Startled, the guard managed to flick on the lights in time to see a garbage can lid flipping around. There was no one in sight, and when he examined the lid, he realized it would take a good solid push to make it move, let alone make it spin around.

Concerned that he had an intruder on his hands, the guard called for backup. He stayed on his radio until the other security guard arrived, and the two hunted through the building together. They found no one. The only way out was through an alarmed fire exit, which would have alerted them to someone leaving. As the two guards prepared to turn off the lights and leave, they heard a sigh from the stairway. Although no one could be seen, the first guard had the distinct impression that someone was standing there, staring at them. The two guards hastily locked up and left.

In December 2001, prior to most of the renovation work, a TGHRS member went to the former hospital site accompanied by a member of Para-Researchers of Ontario. They took photographs inside the buildings, hoping to capture something that might indicate a supernatural presence. They didn't find anything unusual. However, they did hear what they described as a "feminine-sounding moan"—a sound markedly different from the range of natural sounds heard in an empty old building.

The staff at Humber College prefers not to talk about the ghosts. But the stories continue. After all, a place designed to create a restful, restorative home for the mentally ill may have been so pleasant that some of the patients or staff decided to stay on eternally, making it rather unsettling for those who now work there.

The Guild Inn
SCARBOROUGH, ON

High on the Scarborough Bluffs near Toronto, surrounded by lush forest and beautiful statues, is the historic, haunted Guild Inn. With its panoramic view of Lake Ontario, the old hotel has been a favourite spot for weddings and film crews. Famous guests include Kathleen Turner, Sir Laurence Olivier and Christopher Reeve. However, few of the illustrious guests who have stayed at the inn know of the Guild's past, and perhaps current, hauntings. The tranquil, romantic setting definitely has a darker side.

The inn began as a private summer home for Colonel Harold Bickford and his family. Built in 1914, Ranelagh Park, as it was called then, allowed the Bickfords to vacation in style with a nursery, library, nine bedrooms, servants' quarters and large living area. In 1921, Bickford sold the property,

The Scarborough Bluffs are the supernatural backdrop for assorted hauntings at the Guild Inn.

and it became a boarding school for the China Mission Seminary. Two years later, it was sold to another private owner, who renamed it Cliff Acres but rarely enjoyed the location's splendour. From 1932 to 1942 it belonged to Rosa and Spencer Clark, who created a Guild of All Arts and allowed artists to live there in exchange for providing their work to display.

For one year during the war, from 1942 to 1943, the inn became a secret workplace for the Women's Royal Canadian

Naval Service (known as the WRENS). Then, in 1944, the government turned the Guild Inn into a recuperative centre for returning war veterans with nervous disorders. Hundreds of patients spent their days recovering in the peaceful hilltop house until 1947, when it became a public hotel once again.

Krystal Leigh, the granddaughter of a former Guild Inn employee, collaborated with an Ontario paranormal research group to share her grandmother's and her mother's odd experiences as part of an investigation.

Krystal's grandmother worked at the Guild Inn in the 1960s as a banquet waitress. Although no proof existed, other long-time employees who had worked there shortly after the war said that the government had built a tunnel from the Scarborough Bluffs to the main building some distance away. Rumour had it that experiments were conducted in these tunnels during the war. The inn's original blueprints do not show any tunnels, but Krystal said her grandmother used the underground passageways to go back and forth between the main level and the downstairs banquet facilities.

"I have seen bricked-off doorways that may be the access to more tunnels," she writes. "I have been completely alone in the hotel and felt as if I was being watched from the shadows and followed through the narrow corridors."

Krystal's mother worked at the Guild Inn for two decades and experienced many strange things. At the edge of the Bluffs was a small mansion called Cory Cliff, which was built in 1912 and used as a meeting facility. Krystal's mother would arrive early in the mornings to set up the space for the day. She would often hear loud footsteps walking overhead. Knowing that she was completely alone, she would still investigate the source of the noise. She never found anyone. Things continued to happen, such as toilets flushing on their own, doors slamming and taps turning on by themselves. Krystal's mother would leave the building at night after she had turned off every single light. As she walked away from the building, she would see them all come on simultaneously.

More recently, a former employee of the inn named Paul shared his own traumatic experience with the investigators. Since he was one of the last to leave, Paul's routine included cleaning the kitchen, locking the refrigerators and turning off the lights. On one particular night, he'd finished his work and was returning the keys to the front desk when he heard a crash and the distinct sound of the fridge door opening. Since he and the front desk clerk were the only people left in the building, he expected to find his colleague in the kitchen when he investigated the sounds. Instead, Paul found the room empty with the lights on and the refrigerator door wide open. Knowing that he had securely fastened the 12-foot bar and padlock only minutes earlier, Paul was stunned to see the metal bar on the floor and the padlock missing. Paul found the lock on the other side of the kitchen, and as he began to lock the fridge again, he heard someone walking down the hall towards him. Relieved that he was no longer alone, Paul called out to the front desk clerk in hopes of getting an explanation about what happened.

When Paul turned around, instead of the clerk, he found himself face to face with a tall man wearing a black top hat. The man did not appear completely solid, and as if to prove that point, he evaporated before Paul's eyes. Frightened and disbelieving, Paul left the kitchen immediately and never told anyone, except the paranormal group, of his experience for fear of being ridiculed.

On another occasion, a guest staying in the third-floor Spencer Suite came back to find that the drapes he had purposefully drawn closed were pulled open. In his two-night stay, he and other members of his party heard noises coming from other floors that were supposed to be empty. One person also claimed to have seen a lady in a long blue period dress drifting down one of the halls.

Prompted by the reports of strange goings-on, investigators made several trips to the inn. On the first occasion, in September 2001, a team of four investigators and two "sensitives" explored the underground tunnel area. The tunnels don't need anything paranormal to make them creepy. With their low pipes, broken tiles, spider webs and the smell of rotting earth and mildew, there is a sense of despair and abandonment in the dark passages. As the group explored, one of the team saw something huddled in a corner that she could only describe as "a dark, huddled humanish mass." The two women with psychic abilities also detected the entity, and they worked in tandem to communicate with it. Though this was a new way of working for the pair, they ultimately persuaded it, with gentle verbal guidance, to pass on to the spirit realm.

The team's second visit later the same month was an overnight mission. Although their photographs and audio recordings did not pick up any anomalies, one member of the group heard footsteps in an empty attic area.

In October, the researchers booked overnight rooms, and members of the Toronto Ghosts and Hauntings Research Society joined them. One person reported being bothered in the middle of the night by a young man with one blue eye and one brown eye. Her experience was corroborated by reports from a hotel resident who had been plagued by strange dreams of a man with two differently coloured eyes. Other hotel guests on the sixth floor said they'd heard banging in the early morning hours and witnessed door handles turning between adjoining rooms. The guests on either side of the shared rooms made the logical assumption that the noise and rattling doorknobs came from each other's rooms, but when they met at breakfast, they realized that neither side had made the racket.

At checkout time, one of the paranormal investigators noticed her jewellery was missing. It had been on the dresser under some gloves, but the gloves were undisturbed. After a thorough search of the room, they could find no jewellery. Frustrated, the woman voiced aloud her wish that the jewellery be returned. She then spotted the missing property neatly placed on the bed, which she claimed she had already checked.

Cory Cliff was torn down in 1997 because it became too dilapidated to restore. The same fate may await the Guild Inn. It now sits empty after closing to the public in October 2001, and there is talk of tearing it down because the cost of renovation is too high. Meanwhile, Sue Darroch and Para-Researchers of Ontario are still interested in hearing other stories because so few records exist of the ghostly activity at the old inn.

Who are the spirits in the inn? Who is the lady in blue? Any clues might help to deduce the answers. If you have any information, contact PRO via their website: www.pararesearchers.org.

The Homeless Ghost
HAMILTON, ON

Of the many theories about what constitutes a ghost, one suggests that a ghost is a person who died and metaphorically "missed the bus" to the next stop, becoming a stranded spirit. That such lost souls remain among the living is sad enough, but as one worker at a Hamilton homeless shelter discovered, it's heart-wrenching to see the pattern continue after death.

The unnamed employee submitted his story to an Ontario-based paranormal research organization in August 2001. At the beginning of the summer, he had a paranormal encounter while waiting at a bus stop. It was 5 PM, and the evening rush hour was under way. The sidewalks seethed with people in a hurry. But one man took his time, and it was this fellow in a blue baseball cap who caught the shelter worker's attention.

"It was a bright day, and an elderly man passed by me," he reports. "He had a distinctive and familiar gait." The man moved slowly and the employee noticed how he cut a path through the crush of commuters so that people moved around him as they hustled homeward.

The old man's familiarity stuck with the shelter worker, gnawing at him, until he suddenly remembered how he knew him.

"I watched him for a few seconds until I looked away at something across the street. Then I realized that the man I was just watching had stayed at the shelter I work in about two weeks previous." The employee couldn't believe his eyes. While staying at the shelter, the elderly man had suffered terrible stomach pains and was found doubled over in pain on the floor. The shelter staff called an ambulance, which took him to the hospital. "The man passed away the next day," recalled the worker. "I'm not sure what the official cause of death was."

Stunned, the worker continued watching the elderly man's seemingly solid form as he wandered behind a bus shelter and out of sight.

"I was about 12 metres from the bus shelter, so I walked towards it, knowing he could go nowhere but down the road, and I would see that." But as the employee rounded the bus shelter, he could see the man was not there. He walked a long way down the block just to be sure, but he could see no sign of the man in the blue baseball cap. "I know he was walking way too slowly for him to have gone very far or for me not to have seen him. He just vanished."

The lost soul had no family as far as any of the homeless shelter workers knew. He lived on the streets and took refuge in shelters from time to time. "I was not his case worker when he stayed at the shelter, so I had only talked to him three or four times. He was very secretive about his life." All he knew was the man was in his 70s and always wore a blue cap with a logo on it.

As for what he saw, the shelter worker is convinced his eyes did not deceive him. "I truly believe that it was his spirit walking the area it knew best."

Upon reflection, one thing stood out as interesting to the witness. "It amazed me how people just walked around him, aware of him but not really noticing him. No one touched him, even in such a big crowd. There was no glow or light around him." That experience corresponds with many other accounts from people who claim to have seen "solid" apparitions, not transparent forms that are clearly of another dimension.

Why is that? No one really knows. Dozens of theories exist with no real conclusions. Perhaps in this instance, the man feared leaving the streets he knew so well for a journey to the unknown. Or maybe he really did miss the bus and finally found it when he went behind the bus shelter. After all, his spirit hasn't been seen since.

The Rattling Door
COLDWATER, ON

The small Simcoe County village of Coldwater has long been a hidden haven for skiers looking for low-cost accommodation when up for a weekend of downhill pleasure at resorts such as Moonstone. Small apartments over stores could be rented at a price that one group of teens in the early 1980s found affordable, so they pooled their money and created a drop-in place for themselves and their friends. For two of the gang, dropping in turned out to be an eerie experience when they encountered what might have been a ghost across the hall.

Ken and Pete were both 18 at the time and had gone up to Coldwater from Aurora for a weekend rendezvous with two girls they met there during a previous party. They arrived on Saturday, and when they climbed the stairs to the suite above the Red and White Store, they found it in a shambles.

A weekend in a rental apartment turned out to be a spooky experience for two young men on vacation.

"It was a mess," says Ken. "A rundown swampy mash pad with bare mattresses on the floor, an old kitchen and no heat. The place was freezing!"

Undeterred, the pair invited the girls to come over for drinks, and they partied until the early hours. The girls left sometime around 2 AM, and Ken and Pete crashed for a few hours.

"We had to leave early because Pete had to work the next day," recalls Ken. "So we were up before sunrise, around 5:30 or 6:00."

It was quite dark in the long, creepy hallway as the two exited the apartment. Ken left first, and in the dim gleam of a bare light bulb hanging from a wire in the hall ceiling, he could just make out a door across the hall.

"The thing that caught my eye was the door handle. It started to rattle hard, as if someone was trying to open it from the other side." To their amazement, they noticed a heavy padlock on the door. "It appeared as though someone had left the room and locked another person in. The rattling persisted, and it was so frightening that we just got out of there."

With shivers running down their spines, Ken and Pete bolted down the long flight of rickety, narrow stairs to the street below and out into the cold winter morning.

"We took off as fast as we could," says Ken.

The strangest part of the story occurred when they told Chuck, one of the other renters, about what had happened. Ken was surprised by what he learned.

"He told us that there was no apartment across the hall and that the door was to a closet."

Ken is convinced some spirit was trapped in that room and perhaps rattled the door to bring attention to its plight.

"I know what I saw, and it didn't make any sense. It wasn't like a wind or a tremor made that door shake the way it did."

Ken says that morning lives in his memory as vividly today as the day it happened. Not long ago, he revisited the apartment and took some shots of the hallway with his digital camera. His pictures did not reveal any paranormal

Frightened by what they saw on the second floor, the guests escaped by bolting down the stairs.

signs, such as orbs or streaks of ectoplasm, but Ken got the distinct feeling that there was a presence in the hallway.

"The hallway is still so scary that I could not bring myself to go all the way up the stairs."

The current owner of the store below didn't say anything to Ken when he asked about ghosts or paranormal activity in the old building. It could be he hasn't witnessed anything, or perhaps he just prefers to let the spirit in the closet remain secret.

The Tunnel Creature
TORONTO, ON

There's a dark underworld in every city that most people rarely think about. It's not the world of mobsters, but the dank catacombs of infrastructure running like capillaries under every street and building. These tunnels and sewers have long been a source of imaginary creatures for television shows that exploit the paranormal. One man in Toronto, however, has had firsthand experience after coming face to face with a strange creature of the underworld.

Ernest told his story—on condition that he would be identified only by his first name—to a *Toronto Sun* reporter who had heard about it from a friend of a friend. In the end, Ernest's story seems credible despite a lack of tangible evidence. You can decide for yourself.

On an August day in 1978, Ernest discovered that one of the kittens was missing from a litter he and his wife, Barbara, had been raising. Concerned about its welfare, Ernest searched the streets and alleys around their Parliament Street apartment. Not far from home, he stumbled on a dark "cave" at the bottom of a narrow walk between Ernest's building and the one next door. Thinking the kitten might have hidden inside, Ernest crawled about 10 feet into the hole. That decision changed his life.

He told the reporter, "I saw a living nightmare that I'll never forget."

With only a small flashlight to illuminate the blackness, Ernest saw a creature unlike any other. He described it as "long and thin, almost like a monkey, three feet long, large teeth, weighing maybe 30 pounds with slate-grey fur." Its eyes were the most distinguishing and disturbing feature, "orange and red, slanted." An artist's rendering of this beast, which accompanied the *Sun* article, resembles another strange animal—the South American Chupacabra. Said to resemble a living gargoyle, that cyptozoological creature supposedly attacks goats and other animals and drinks their blood to survive.

The terrifying creature spoke to Ernest. "It said, 'Go away, go away,' in a hissing voice. Then it took off down a long tunnel off to the side. I got out of there as fast as I could."

Shaking with fear, Ernest returned home to his wife of 19 years with his spine-chilling tale. He didn't want to tell anyone else because he knew it sounded unbelievable. Barbara took in her husband's state, and decided he must be telling the truth.

"I believe Ernie saw exactly what he says he did." She confirmed that he had not been drinking that day and that the experience really shook him. "He was terrified when he came back to the apartment, and he doesn't scare easily."

To follow up, the *Sun* convinced Ernest to return to the "cave" in March 1979. While hunting around, the reporter and Ernest found the corpse of a cat half-buried in the tunnel. It reminded Ernest that he had also heard horrible noises, like those of an animal in pain, emanating from the tunnel before his strange sighting.

No second encounter occurred with the unusual monster. The reporter and Ernest could see that the passageway seemed to be quite long. Could it be that this was a little-known access point to the sewer system and that the creature had used it to sneak up to the earth's surface?

Oddly enough, when interviewed, none of the employees who work in the sewers made fun of Ernest's story. Their comments actually seemed to support his experience.

One worker quoted in the article said, "People who work on the surface just don't know what it's like down there. It's a whole different world." Others stated they would never go down alone.

No other stories have since surfaced about the tunnel creature. Perhaps its one startling confrontation with a human sent it deep into the honeycombed lair of tunnels, where it now waits patiently for a safe time to venture once more to the surface.

2
The Prairies

Who's Scared Now?

WINNIPEG, MB

Kelly was in love. As she looked at Nick, she knew that she had found the man with whom she was going to spend the rest of her life. He was perfect for her, and even after all the time they had spent together, she'd yet to find an unforgivable flaw in his personality. His house, on the other hand, was a completely different matter.

It all happened one night more than 23 years ago in Winnipeg, in a house on Ottawa Avenue.

Kelly, with her sister and a friend in tow, were on their way to Nick's house. He was working, but that was all right. Nick and his friends were going to meet them later. The girls were going to pass the evening playing cards, a quiet night with good friends and good conversation. As Kelly drove, the radio provided background for their animated chatter. But the car fell suddenly silent when Kelly pulled into her boyfriend's driveway.

She couldn't be certain that anyone else saw what she saw: a flash of light, the glimmer of what Kelly later described as a "fluorescent light turning on and off quickly" just by the window of the master bedroom. She blinked, wondering what it was that she had witnessed.

Turning to her sister, Kelly whispered, "Did you see that?"

Her sister answered, "You saw that too?"

At which point the siblings turned their heads to the back seat, and their friend whispered, "You both saw that?"

"We were all surprised that we had seen the same thing," Kelly said.

They sat in the car wondering what they had seen. Finally, Kelly hit on a hypothesis. She reasoned that what they had seen was nothing other than her car's headlights reflected back to them by power lines. To test her theory, Kelly backed out of the driveway, drove around the block and came back to the house. But no flash of light met their eyes this time.

Shaking their heads, they got out of the car. Kelly looked skyward, hoping to see power lines stretched out above her. No power lines.

The episode might have faded quickly from their memories were it an isolated incident, but the minute the girls entered the house, they felt that something was not quite right. Everything felt a little different, out of the ordinary, including Nick's two timber wolves. Normally quite docile and gregarious, the two were agitated and hostile, barking and baring their teeth as the girls walked in through the front door.

"Go lie down," Kelly commanded. "Go." The animals seemed to relax and padded off to a bedroom. Kelly frowned. "They aren't usually aggressive animals," she said.

The girls turned on some music and sat down at the kitchen table to play cards. They pushed the night's strange incidents from their minds and were soon engaged in lively conversation that had little to do with strange lights and pets. Their comfort, however, was brief.

Above their heads, the girls heard something entirely odd coming from the master bedroom. They were startled from their card game when the house was filled with the sound of loud squeaks and creaks. Their eyes opened wide with fear. Was someone in the house with them?

"It was as if someone was pulling furniture across the floor upstairs," Kelly said.

Frightened, the girls wondered what they should do. They debated in hushed voices about whether one or all of the girls should go upstairs and check the rooms, but the discussion ended abruptly when one of Nick's dogs walked into the main room. The girls looked at each other and then at the dog. They smiled and shook their heads in unison.

"We decided to send the dogs upstairs," Kelly said. "They're timber wolves. If an intruder was up there, I'd sure feel sorry for the intruder."

But their plan hit a snag. Just as when they had first entered the house, the dogs became agitated and refused to obey any commands. The two dogs sat stubbornly at the bottom of the stairs, refusing to climb them.

"I was really surprised," Kelly marvelled. "We used to play hide-and-seek with them all the time, and they never had a problem going anywhere. They'd rush all over the place. But that night, they just wouldn't go upstairs." Of course, if these animals, which still depended to a degree upon their instincts for their survival, weren't going to brave the unknown upstairs, then neither was Kelly or any of her friends.

Looking back, Kelly remembers being scared. "I don't know why we didn't leave the house," she says. In the end, perhaps it was because she remembered that the master bedroom was carpeted, which made her realize that whoever or whatever was making the scraping sounds couldn't be real.

Besides, any intruder leaving the house would have to get past the three girls who were seated near the front door. Also, Kelly realized that Nick and his friends would be home soon. The girls just sat together and waited. When the men came home, the girls asked them to search the house, which they did, revealing no unwelcome intruders.

Yet when her future husband asked to hear what had happened, Kelly was surprised when they received a less-than-sympathetic reaction. As the women told their story, the men stared, incredulous.

With a laugh, they dismissed everything that had happened. "You're just being crazy," Nick said. "Do you really think it was a ghost? There's no such thing. That's just stupid."

Feeling a little foolish and disappointed that she wasn't being taken seriously, Kelly refused to believe that what she had experienced might be the result of an overactive imagination. After all, if that was the case, then how could Nick account for her sister and friend sharing the same story? Mass hysteria was the answer. Kelly cast a withering smile at her boyfriend as if to say, *Hey, it's your house, not mine, so it's your ghost and not mine.*

The rest of the night passed without incident but with much teasing at the expense of Kelly and her friends. The irony, of course, was that while she had been terrified earlier and had wanted nothing more than a return to normalcy, now Kelly was hoping that the phenomenon would return and stand as proof of her account. But, alas, it seemed as if the spirit had decided to withdraw. Kelly returned home, convinced that she would be vindicated. She didn't have to wait long.

Just days later, Kelly received an early morning phone call from her boyfriend. The fog of slumber soon dissipated when she heard her boyfriend's panicked voice. Although empathetic, Kelly couldn't resist allowing herself a little smirk of self-satisfaction as she listened to what he had to say.

Her husband-to-be told her that he had gone to bed the evening before, only to wake up and find himself at the mercy of an invisible being. He didn't know what was assaulting him but knew that something was pushing down on his chest. His strength failed him; he found it impossible to rise from his bed. His muscles strained and strained, but he just couldn't get up. His eyes were open wide, taking in the reality that a non-corporeal being was attacking him. A bellow issued forth from his mouth, and he wrenched himself free of the bed with one last Herculean effort. He stared at the bed, stunned. Had it really happened? Now that something inexplicable had happened to him, he couldn't help thinking now that maybe his fiancée was right. Maybe something strange was going on in his house. He reached for his phone and dialled Kelly's number.

The incident may have motivated Nick to ask Kelly to move in with him before they got married. They were in the house when he asked her. Kelly told him that she would need to think it over; it's not every day that someone asks you to move into a haunted house. Kelly loved Nick and would have loved to wake up next to him not just every so often, but every day. But the house terrified her. She had almost made her decision when Nick approached her one day.

"Hey, why'd you take these papers out?" he asked, waving some forms in his hand.

Kelly looked at them. She shook her head. "I didn't take those out."

"Well, somebody did. Because I sure didn't. And if you didn't…" Nick's voice trailed off, and his eyes met Kelly's. In them, he saw recognition, a winking understanding that the two knew what had been responsible for taking the papers out.

"No." Kelly smiled. "I won't be moving into this house."

Nick nodded. He understood completely.

After they were married, the couple moved away from the house on Ottawa Avenue. The two dogs came with them. Kelly remembered their knack for predicting the unpredictable and thought they could determine whether the new house was haunted before they bought it. Thankfully, their new house has been ghost-free.

When asked if she has ever returned to the house on Ottawa Avenue, Kelly laughs.

"No. I've never gone back. I don't want the ghosts to know that we're still around. They might follow us home. We've got friends who live near the house. We've never told them about the ghosts. We just don't want them to know that we're around."

A Partridge, a Pear Tree and a Ghost
WINNIPEG, MB

Jean Gillingham can't be entirely sure, but she believes that the house numbered 536 is one of the oldest on the street, dating back at least 80 years. She has lived in it for more than 40 years, and during that time she has raised and nurtured a family, loved and lost a husband and nursed and lost a mother. Jean lives in the house alone now, but she is never starved for company. Her grandchildren come by often, and Jean continues to enrich and enliven the tapestry that is her family. And when the grandchildren leave the house, there is the ghost to keep Jean company, a spirit that has been with the Gillinghams almost from the time they began to call 536 Victoria Avenue home.

She can't recall the exact moment that she first realized she had a visitor from the afterlife in her house, but Jean has become accustomed to waking in the morning with a sense of anticipation as she wonders what object will be misplaced, what items will be rearranged and which pieces of furniture will be disturbed. Jean recalls most of the incidents fondly, amusement and surprise strong in her voice.

"I've never been too worried about what's happened. I'm not a nervous person anyway, and as long as they don't do anything bad, I don't worry." Of course Jean has no idea who *they* are. She has never seen a ghost or heard one, but what she has seen is enough to confirm her belief in paranormal visitations.

One of her daughters did see something once, a girl "sitting on a bed with her legs swinging." She asked the apparition what she was doing there but the girl just disappeared. The sighting was a rarity. More often, Jean is made aware of a ghost's presence through paranormal incidents. These incidents may have taken place years ago, but Jean can still recall them with clarity and precision.

Most people get excited for the Christmas season because they look forward to the holidays, the long-awaited arrivals of rarely seen relatives and the festivities, food and gifts that accompany them. They cherish the goodwill of the season, and the laughter of children dancing under softly falling snow. Jean loves Christmas too, but she has entirely different reasons to get excited.

"Strange things happen at Christmas," she recalls.

One holiday season, as the family prepared to decorate the tree, boxes of decorations were dutifully brought out of storage. The boxes were opened, and carefully packed ornaments were lovingly removed from their wrappings, dusted off and displayed on the tree.

Jean reached inside a box and pulled out another. Inside were five velvet birds that had quickly become a holiday favourite when they were first bought. Jean let out an exclamation. Concerned family members came over to see what had happened. Jean pulled out the five birds, showing everyone that the head of each one had come off.

"The heads had been severed," Jean says. "It really was the strangest thing. We wondered if insects might have done the damage, but they had been packed inside the box I'd bought them in and then in another box. Would insects have chewed through two boxes? I don't think so." But Jean didn't let the event rattle her. Since she was a teacher, she went to her students with the story and had them write ghost stories about what had happened to her birds. As students will, they came up with some imaginative stories to explain the unexplainable.

Christmases came and went, and at the conclusion of each, the Gillingham family always had some new and strange event to discuss. One year, Jean had knit a pair of thick, bulky wool socks for her son-in-law. She placed the finished socks in a closet on a shelf until her son-in-law came over to receive his gift. But when he arrived and she went to retrieve them, the socks were gone. At first, she thought she might have misplaced them, but her son-in-law was well over six feet tall and the socks were large to match; they weren't easily misplaced. Then she thought that perhaps someone had stolen them. Jean stopped herself.

"Who would ever take a pair of socks?" she asked. And in order for someone to take the socks, they would have to break into the house. No one had.

It seems as if the spirit strongly dislikes the idea of Jean making clothing for her family. Jean remembers another year when she had bought three metres of red velveteen fabric to make a Christmas costume for her grandchild. Returning home, she put the fabric in her toy room for later use. When she came back to find the velveteen, it had disappeared. To this day, the fabric's whereabouts remain a mystery.

But the spirit's inclinations do not lean strictly to clothing. The being has sometimes offered Jean unsolicited serving suggestions. Take, for example, the night that Jean peeled about 40 cloves of garlic for a dinner she was preparing the next day.

Jean put the peeled cloves in a bowl on the kitchen counter, and she and her husband went up to bed. The next morning, when Jean awoke, her husband had already padded downstairs to make breakfast. When she got into the kitchen, she laughed and shook her head.

"What did you do that for?" she asked her husband. There, on the kitchen counter, were the 40 cloves of garlic. "They were lined up, end to end, like a train."

Her husband turned and looked at her. He smiled and then pointed at the garlic cloves. "What? That? I didn't do that."

Jean shrugged. There might have been a time when she would have accused her husband of pulling her leg, but that time was long past. The two had spent the night by themselves; who else could it have been? Who knows? It might have been her husband all along. But then, two years ago, her husband passed away, leaving Jean alone in the house.

One morning when she awoke, Jean walked by the living room and then stopped. With brow furrowed and mind puzzled, Jean turned around and looked at the floor. No, she hadn't imagined it. There really was a doll sitting in the living room doorway. How did it get there? Jean did keep her dolls in the living room but on the other side of the room. She rarely went into the living room now, only going in when she needed a phone book. She couldn't recall taking a doll from her collection and standing it in the doorway.

"Had it been there before, I would have noticed," Jean reasons, thinking that perhaps one of her grandchildren had put it there. "But the night before, everything was in order. It's funny too because it's the Claudia doll. My grandchildren named it that because it resembles an evil girl they saw in a movie. Some grandchildren also refuse to sleep in that room because of it."

If neither she nor her grandchildren moved the doll, then Jean was convinced it must have been the spirit. And while she has no idea who the spirit might be, Jean is sure that the ghost means no harm. Like a child, it is mischievous, and she can recall only one time when she might have been bothered or upset by what the spirit had done.

Almost 30 years ago, Jean's mother was staying at the house. One evening, her mother and her husband had gone out for the evening. Jean had fallen asleep early, but for some reason, she woke up at midnight. She went to see if her mother had come home yet, and she heard papers rustling in the living room. The light was on.

"Mum, is that you? Are you home?" Jean called out. The sleepy daughter couldn't help but wonder why anyone was in the rarely used living room. Maybe her mother didn't want to wake her as she read the paper. Jean turned the corner and walked into the room. On the chesterfield, a newspaper was spread out. Otherwise the room was empty.

"It bothered me," Jean said. "The house was locked up. I was very uneasy. There hadn't even been a newspaper in that room, and I was alone in the house."

Understandably, Jean quizzed her mother the next morning. She wanted to be absolutely certain that it wasn't her mother who had been reading the newspaper late into the evening. Of course it wasn't. Her mother hadn't returned to the house until after 1 AM and had gone to bed immediately. Once again Jean felt the unease and dread that had been her companions the night before. Nevertheless, Jean is grateful to have been frightened only once in a lifetime of hauntings.

"Nothing has ever harmed me," she said. "They're just little tricks."

However, it doesn't seem as if one can live in a haunted house unscathed, untouched or unaffected. Jean can't be sure, but she does have her suspicions that she might be haunted not only by an unknown spirit, but also by one dear to her heart.

"They might be my dreams," Jean said. "But I feel as if I've seen my husband twice. Once, it felt like he was standing by my bed. I asked him why I couldn't fall asleep."

Jean still lives at 536 Victoria Avenue. She lives alone, but her family and at least one anonymous spirit make sure that she is never lonely.

"I've never seen or heard a ghost," Jean said, "but there must be someone there."

Not Your Average Childhood
SHILO, MB

Autumn never really believed in ghosts. By nature, she questioned the unexplained, believing that a logical and reasonable explanation would eventually present itself. But that was before one eerie evening that, even after more than a decade, resists her best attempts to explain it without uttering the word "ghost."

"A lot of the details are hazy," Autumn writes. "I was younger when this happened. I've forgotten a lot." What Autumn is left with, then, are impressions and emotions she still feels keenly. All she needs to do to travel back in time is recall the fear and dread that gripped her heart when she was a child growing up in the tightly knit military town of Shilo, Manitoba, on streets like Kingston Road, lined with military-style duplexes.

For many years, she never said a word to anyone about what happened and has yet to confide in her family. In her opinion, her devout Christian parents would be less than receptive to her experiences.

"Heaven forbid their child should experience anything abnormal," she writes. "I was afraid to say anything…people would say I was being ridiculous." Answers to her questions, then, have been in short supply.

The night in question took place in 1987, when Autumn was five years old. Her days were filled with play and the carefree ease of innocent youth. Each day, she was roused out of bed at 6 AM by her mother and taken down, with eyes still bleary and head still foggy with sleep, to the breakfast table to

eat. After breakfast, there was just enough time for shower-
ing, brushing her teeth and running a comb through her tousled hair. It didn't really matter, of course. By the time she got
back from kindergarten at noon, in time for lunch, her hair
was just as tousled as ever. And anyway, the rest of the day
was hers to do with as she pleased. Her options weren't many,
but they didn't need to be at a time when the backyard or a
friend's house were rife with possibilities. She would play
until it was time for dinner. After dinner, Autumn would play
with her sister or lie on her mother's lap as they watched television. Then it was off to bed, where Autumn would drift off
to sleep, eager and ready to greet another day. At least that
was how it was supposed to be.

One night, having settled blissfully into sleep, Autumn
was roused from her slumber. To her wide-eyed terror, she
saw a figure seated at the end of her bed.

"I was terrified," she says. "I tried to scream and found
myself unable to speak. My mouth moved soundlessly."
Autumn was at the mercy of the glimmering figure. She
guessed that it was a woman because of the figure's long hair,
but other distinguishing features were obscured by the figure's pure luminescence.

"It was wearing robes made of light," Autumn explains. "A
bright white light." She tried closing her eyes to shield herself
from its brilliance, but it made no difference. It was like trying to shut out the sun. The figure didn't threaten the young
girl; it just sat at the foot of the bed, hovering just above
Autumn's quilt. It observed the terrified child with eyes so
focused and intent that she felt as if they "were peering into
my soul."

Autumn looked around the room desperately for anything that might help her, but even that proved too much for her. The room, once familiar and comforting, had become cold and strange.

"The room got darker," Autumn recalls. "It seemed to change, as if every object was being influenced by the figure's presence. Everything seemed altered in a strange way. It wasn't totally threatening but it was changed."

The figure probably appeared for only the briefest of moments, but to Autumn the glowing light hovered above her bed for what seemed like a lifetime. The moment did pass, however, and Autumn found herself again alone in her bedroom. She lay in her bed, shaking with fear and trying to understand the experience, eyes tightly scrunched as if to shut it out. She doesn't remember how long she lay in bed scared and confused, but she awoke the next morning cradled in her mother's arms. Her mother told Autumn that she had crawled into bed with her during the night.

Years later, Autumn continues to reflect upon that night in Shilo. She still has no idea who or what might have appeared to her in her bedroom that night but she is willing to hazard some guesses. She is convinced now that what she saw was an angel.

Asked why, she answers, "I was convinced because that's what I always imagined angels to look like." But she has no idea why an angel might have appeared to her. She can't remember anything about the day previous to the apparition's appearance that marked it as unusual.

"I was a happy child," she says. "That day wasn't any different. I had no problems. And I'm pretty sure the house isn't built on a burial ground or anything obvious like that."

Complicating matters is that Autumn appears to be the only person to whom the angel appeared. Other residents of Shilo, who also have stories to tell, have no experiences similar to Autumn's.

The experience was far from life altering. "I'm not sure if much changed," Autumn writes. "I was so young when it happened that I'm not able to compare things from before and after the incident. I do dream about things to come, and many have come true but I don't know if I've always had them." And, of course, she must have had other things on her mind. Her father came to her a year later and said, "We're moving to a big city."

Autumn never saw the apparition again and is quite certain that she's the only one to have seen it. Not long after, her family moved to Victoria. There, her biggest concern was how she would adjust to life in a city. It was an adjustment to be sure, but while Autumn progressed through childhood into her teens and then young adulthood she never forgot that evening in Shilo when an unknown angel intruded upon her world of school and play.

Incredibly, when she was 11, she had another eerie experience.

Autumn was out collecting golf balls on a golf course. She liked finding the balls that other golfers were just too lazy to retrieve, placing them in egg cartons for ease in carrying, and then selling them back to golfers who didn't want to pay full price for new balls. It was lucrative but it could also be messy work.

The rains had poured from the skies for a week, turning the greens and the grounds of the golf course into a bog. Autumn found herself walking ankle deep in mud and grass, sucking sounds accompanying her every step. The weather was discouraging, but Autumn and a friend pressed on, determined to add to the meagre number of balls they'd managed to collect that day. They went farther afield in their search for the balls, until they were on the outskirts of the cemetery around which the golf course had been built. Although it was eerie being so close to a resting place for the dead, Autumn and her friend pushed on.

As the hours passed, however, their resolve began to fade, and the two decided to split up in order to cover more ground. After five minutes, they would meet again and then leave. The skies were beginning to darken, and as disturbing as the graveyard was during the day, in the evening it would be much worse. Autumn realized later that she left the graveyard five minutes too late.

As her friend walked off to her left, Autumn approached a stand of trees just opposite the cemetery. Something caught her attention, and it wasn't a golf ball. High above the ground, dangling from a tree, was a shadowy figure. The sight was terrifying. Autumn could think only of running to find her friend.

Her face was ashen and her body trembled. Autumn's voice quivered as she told her friend about what she had seen. Her friend's reaction was riddled with skepticism.

"You're just being a scaredy cat," her friend said. "You probably just let your imagination run crazy." But her friend insisted on seeing the sight for herself. And so the two girls crept back through the sticky mud towards the stand of trees. Crouching behind bushes, Autumn hazarded a peek at the tree. There was no doubt in her mind now; it had nothing to do with her imagination. The figure was still there, silhouetted against the darkening sky. She heard her friend gasp, and then the two were silent. They watched the figure for a time and then ran home where their stories were met with further skepticism. Children were known, after all, for their overactive imaginations.

As the sun rose to signal the beginning of another day, Autumn and her friend returned to the cemetery to see if the figure was still there. In the rosy pink of the dawn, the girls saw nothing but the tree. Even more remarkable was that the ground beneath the tree was undisturbed. If someone had indeed been hanged on the tree, then wouldn't there be tracks in the rain-soaked ground? Autumn could certainly see her tracks from the night before.

"Don't you see?" her friend said. "That wasn't a person. It was something else."

For Autumn, that much was obvious. She stopped collecting golf balls for a while and felt something that she hadn't felt in a long time: wonder and awe at a world that was not always explainable.

St. Louis Lights
ST. LOUIS, SK

Samantha, or Sammy as she's known to her closest friends, was bored. She was tired of studying, having already spent the last couple of hours poring over dusty journals and worn texts in the reading room at the Rutherford Library on the University of Alberta campus in Edmonton. Her eyes were sore, weary from a day of reading and jotting down notes. Originally she had planned on spending the night studying, but the prospect began to grow less and less appealing as the minutes plodded by. She yawned and slammed her textbooks shut.

Sammy abandoned the reading room and went to find herself a drink heavy with caffeine. A smile broke across her face when she spied her friend, Jen, waiting to pay for a magazine. Jen would have something to do that would take her mind off statistics and English literature, if only for a while. Sammy wasn't disappointed.

Jen was from Saskatchewan, near the town of St. Louis, about 130 kilometres northeast of Saskatoon. The two had met after suffering through their first statistics class together, and Jen had told Sammy about St. Louis and her trips to its "haunted track." Now, with the weekend on its way, Jen and some of her friends were primed and ready to make the drive to St. Louis to experience its legendary ghost train.

Sammy laughed. She couldn't believe that her friends could be so gullible and naive.

"You're serious? You guys are really going to go drive out there to see a ghost train?"

The St. Louis Lights, possibly the manifestation of a ghost train, have perplexed many visitors to the Saskatchewan town.

"Hey," Jen answered. "Road trip. Why not? You should come with us. Forget about the homework for a while."

Sammy thought about it. She wasn't really thrilled about going to St. Louis just to see some lights in the sky, but a road trip was a road trip. It had been a while since she'd been out of Edmonton, and getting away might be a good idea.

"Yeah, why not? I'll go."

Jen smiled. "It's going to be fun."

A few hours later, chilled by the cold of an Edmonton winter night, Jen, Sammy and their friends piled into a car loaded down with an assortment of CDs, potato chips and drinks and began the six-hour journey east to Saskatchewan.

Time passed quickly. The conversation was boisterous and jovial, and the hot chocolate warmed their blood. Despite the chill in the air, it was a beautiful night. The skies were clear, and the moon and stars cast a blue light on the snow-blanketed land. Sammy couldn't help thinking that, once they'd left streetlights behind, being in the car with nothing but headlights to illuminate their way would be a little disconcerting. And it was. Beyond the arcs of light from the headlights, the night was pitch black. But that was part of the fun. Wasn't it?

When they reached the rural area outside St. Louis, Jen drove the car alongside an old railway track, ignoring the many "No Trespassing" signs that had been erected to divert them from their path. Sammy watched out the rear window as the signs were swallowed by the night. Conversation in the car ceased, and everyone fell silent as anticipation gave way to anxiety. Jen had been regaling them for hours with stories about her encounters with what was known locally as the St. Louis Lights. She talked about an article she'd read, proclaiming that two high school students from La Ronge, Saskatchewan, had solved the mystery of the St. Louis Lights.

According to the students' theory, the lights came from the headlights of cars passing along a hilltop section of Highway No. 2, about 9 kilometres away. To contest the claim that there is no way that the lights could appear so brightly and prominently from such a distance, they turned to the principle of diffraction—that light passing through a relatively small opening, say gaps between stands of trees, will diffuse and expand in size, becoming visible at great distances. Jen dismissed the students' theory. She pointed to the endurance of the St. Louis Lights, how residents have witnessed the lights during the day and how accounts of the lights date from a time before cars and their headlights were a common sight on the windswept prairies.

To be sure, the accounts were exciting and more than a little frightening. And despite what Sammy believed about the existence of ghosts and manifestations of the paranormal, she had to admit that she was a little scared.

The car rolled to a stop, snow crunching under the tires. Sammy and her friends spilled out of the car, and they cast their wary gazes towards the horizon. Their frosty breath scarcely had a chance to fade into nothingness before they saw the light.

It started out simply enough—just two lights, looking like nothing more than a car's headlights approaching in the distance. Then the two spheres of light merged into one and split apart, only to repeat the process over and over again with increased urgency. As the lights bobbed up and down across the horizon, the young people decided to leave. They tried to race back to their car to get away but the deep snow prevented them. The car's tires spun helplessly. And all the while, the eerie lights came ever closer, glowing ever brighter.

"Someone's going to have to push," Jen said, her voice urgent and desperate.

Sammy nodded. She got out with another friend, and the two began to push. The car rolled back into the rut it had carved out for itself. They pushed again. It rolled back again. Sammy looked over her shoulder at the lights; they'd intensified to such a brilliance that she had to turn away.

"Come on, come on," she hissed, as she continued to push the car.

The lights were getting closer, and they had undergone a metamorphosis. The spheres had become one glowing orb, surrounded by little pinpricks of red light.

The car lurched free, and Sammy fell to the ground. She looked up and saw the red rear lights of the car pull away from her. She scrambled to her knees, trying to rise to her feet. She gasped. Something was gripping her ankle. Sammy opened her mouth to scream, but to her horror she couldn't make a sound. Tears streamed down her face as she contorted her face, hoping with each second that she would be able to cry out for help. Her whole world bled red as the orb of light winked out, leaving just the little red lights to bob and weave through the air like fireflies. All Sammy knew was that she wanted to get away from the red lights that seemed almost close enough for her to touch.

"Just let me go," she thought, pleading with the unknown force. "Just let me go back to my friends." Without warning, Sammy was released, pitched backwards to the snow.

"It was like playing tug of war and the other side suddenly lets go," she later explained to her friends.

Finally free, Sammy wiped the tears from her face with her mittened hands and ran towards the car. With everyone now inside, it raced down the tracks, past the very same "No Trespassing" signs they had ignored on their way in. Only when they were clear of St. Louis did they allow themselves a sigh of relief.

The mood on their return journey was far more subdued. Sammy and Jen sat wearily in the front seat. The CD player was silent, and for six hours all they could talk about was what had happened. They all agreed that Sammy had suffered the worst of it, although none could decide why.

Privately, Sammy cursed her skepticism. It was her disbelief, after all, that had separated her from Jen and the others. She couldn't help thinking that something in St. Louis must have sensed her doubt and had chosen to prove her wrong. She allowed herself a scornful laugh. The experience had driven all doubt about the existence of the paranormal world from her mind. As she returned to her room, Sammy was never happier to see her textbooks. Economics and statistics might be dull and tedious, but at least they were safe.

Sammy's experience affected her deeply. She couldn't think of that frigid winter evening without breaking into a cold sweat, her body stiffening and her heart racing. Shadows became threatening, even menacing. To conquer her fears, she decided to return to St. Louis and tempt fate once again.

Sammy left for St. Louis with a different set of friends and was unable to keep her frayed nerves calm during the six-hour drive. They arrived at the tracks and got out of the car, acquainted with Sammy's stories and aware of how the bright white lights are believed to be the lights of an old steam locomotive. The smaller red ones are those of people searching for the head of a conductor who had the misfortune to be decapitated while performing a routine inspection of the tracks.

Sammy was overwhelmed with a strange sensation and returned to the car without waiting to see what happened.

She couldn't be sure what she had felt, but she knew it didn't feel right. Her feelings were confirmed when her friends returned to the car heavy with fear. She didn't even ask them what they had seen. She was pretty sure that she didn't want to hear it.

"The ghosts are out there," she said. "You don't really want them to prove it."

Sammy learned that lesson the hard way on that cold winter's night. Once skeptical, Sammy no longer doubts the existence of the paranormal. Asked if she would ever return, Sammy just shakes her head. A third trip to St. Louis is highly unlikely.

A Strange and Gifted Life
WINNIPEG, MB

Cory's life, to put it simply, is far from normal. While most people live their lives unsure of what might lie beyond the physical realm and are content to pursue financial security and its attendant freedoms, Cory moves through the world acutely aware of forces that defy comprehension and logic. She possesses an intuition and sensitivity that may frighten some, intrigue others, but engage everyone. Her fascinating talents revealed themselves when she was a very young child in Winnipeg.

"I've had many experiences in my life," Cory says. So many that she is unable to recall that epiphanous moment when she knew that her life would be unlike any other. She recalls her mother telling her that she was a precocious child who could sense events before they happened.

Cory woke up one morning, unable to shake the feeling that something was amiss and that she needed to call her family. For Cory, it was an unusual sensation. Although she was close to her family, she didn't call them or speak with them all that often. She just couldn't understand the compulsion on that morning to call her family, but she couldn't ignore the gnawing sense of dread that something horrible had happened.

Her husband, tired and weary, mumbled, "It's too early to be calling them."

Cory nodded. She made herself a cup of tea instead and sat by the phone. And then the phone rang. It was 8:00. With

A remarkable ability to predict bingo winners is only one of the skills of a highly sensitive Manitoba woman.

slightly trembling hands, Cory picked up the receiver. It was her cousin, and even though she already knew the answer to the question she was going to ask, she asked it anyway.

"Someone's died. Hasn't he?"

In a voice muffled with tears and loss, Cory's cousin asked, "How did you know? Uncle Tommy died last night."

Cory's husband quickly became accustomed to his wife's peculiar abilities, but he still often found himself a little frightened. Take, for example, the time when he and his wife shook hands with their lawyer. The couple were riding down in the elevator when Cory turned to her husband and said, in a matter-of-fact way, "You just shook the hand of a dead man."

Her husband became agitated and shuffled from foot to foot uncomfortably. "Don't say that. He'll be fine. I mean, he looked fine, didn't he?"

Cory just stared up at her husband with a pitiful glance and shook her head. Days later, the couple learned that their lawyer had indeed passed away the day after they had seen him.

"I'm never frightened by what I see," Cory says. "I've lived with it all my life, and like most things, you just have to accept it. It's weird, sure." Even when she was a child, Cory never questioned the weird things that happened in her life.

"If a voice told me to do things, I'd do it," she recounts as she describes the first paranormal incident that she can remember.

She doesn't remember her exact age but she was young and playing with a friend in a trailer just a little more than half a mile from her parents' house. Somewhere inside her head, Cory heard a voice telling her to run home.

"I've got to go home," she said to her friend.

"Why? Don't go."

"I have to."

Little Cory took off down the street, running the entire way. When she finally got home, short of breath, she found her mother sitting on the front steps of their home, cradled in the arms of Cory's sisters. Her shoulders were shaking, and tears streamed down her face. Cory could barely make out the words above her mother's sobs, but she was able to discern amid the grief that her father had died.

A short time later, while living in the Gilbert Park Developments, Cory was watching television alone while her mother and stepfather were asleep upstairs. She knew it was a foolish thing to do, but it was just easier to leave the doors unlocked, as her family did. Her brothers and sisters weren't home yet, and when they returned, they wouldn't have to fish for keys.

So when Cory heard another voice inside her head telling her to run, she knew that it couldn't have been anyone from her family that she heard. She paused, wanting to make sure that she had really heard the voice. When it spoke again, again commanding her to run, Cory wasted no time. She turned off the television and ran up the stairs and into her bedroom.

She heard someone enter the house through the back door and walk down the steps into the living room, where she had just been watching television. Cory assumed it was someone from her family returning, and she bounded back to the living room stairs, calling out her family's names. No response. From the top of the stairs, she saw a man whom she had never seen before walking back and forth, stopping in front of the chair Cory had vacated just moments earlier.

"He had the strangest eyes," Cory recalled. "They were glazed and he just kept saying, 'Audrey, Audrey.'"

Cory had no desire to find out who Audrey was, and she yelled at the stranger to get out of the house. Her yelling roused her stepfather from sleep, and he came out of the bedroom to investigate the disturbance. Once the stranger saw Cory's stepfather, he fled from the house.

An otherworldly presence seems to be making itself known in this Christmas photo.

Cory is convinced that the voice saved her from certain harm.

"The first place he went to was where I was watching television. If I hadn't run, and he did something, no one would have heard me. Everyone was fast asleep." Cory will never know for certain what might have happened that evening, but she is content not to know. She has other more pressing matters on her mind, after all.

Not too long ago, two people that Cory knew decided to take their lives. Both were close to her son. One was an ex-girlfriend and the other was a cousin, who'd been a rough kid but who had always treated her epileptic son with care and compassion. The cousin put a gun against his head and pulled the trigger. Nine months later, the ex-girlfriend took her life. The deaths cut deeply and may have set in motion a flurry of paranormal activity.

While the lights in Cory's house had always flickered off and on, the phenomenon always seemed bound to the house. After the suicides, however, Cory noticed a disturbing trend. Lights everywhere, not just in the house, flickered off and on.

"Wherever I went," Cory said, "where I would walk, lights went off and on."

Pulling into the back lane behind her house, the street-lights would transform into strobe lights. If she went into her basement, the sickly light that hung in the corner did the same.

Driving home with her husband one day, Cory appro-ached a bridge that had been completed just months earlier. As they drove, Cory told her husband about what had been happening.

"Cory," he said. "You know I don't like hearing about this."

"But it's so bizarre, isn't it?" Cory asked.

The car crossed the bridge that was illuminated by newly installed streetlights. As the car made its way across the span, Cory and her husband held their breaths in nervous antici-pation. Would the lights stay on? Cory's husband looked at his wife with resignation as soon as the first of the lights went out and then came back on. The others followed in succes-sion as if they were experiencing an electrical short.

"I told you," Cory said. "Didn't I tell you this would happen?"

Even after the lights had calmed down somewhat, Cory still wasn't free of whatever forces the suicides might have disturbed. Lights aside, her television soon began behaving strangely as well.

"It was Christmas," she says. "I was feeling ill about these deaths." She found comfort in the company of her children and foster children and was able to forget for a moment the tragedies of the past year as she watched her family open their presents. The lights in the room had decided to behave normally and bathed the room in their warm glow. Then the television suddenly went on.

Cory turned from her rocking chair to look around the room. Who had turned it on? She looked at her foster son on the chair behind her, but he just stared back. Her other foster son, sitting on the floor in a sea of wrapping paper, peered up from his presents and gazed from mother to brother, their faces asking the same perplexing question: how did the television turn on? Maybe it was the remote?

"There is no remote control for it," Cory explains. "The only way to turn that television on was to do it manually." Cory was in for more surprises when she saw the photographs she'd taken over the holidays.

Cory had used the two or three exposures left on the roll to take pictures of her house and its Christmas decorations. When she went to pick up the developed photos, she also took a disposable camera that her husband had found at the bottom of a cupboard. It had only four exposures left. As she walked away from her house and to her car, Cory snapped more shots of the house.

She dropped off the new roll and picked up her photographs. Looking through them, she wondered why all but the last three had turned out all right. She couldn't quite explain what was wrong with the last three, but it looked as if the room was covered in a mist or fog.

"Excuse me," she said to the film technician, "but did someone drop something on the film?" The technician looked puzzled and examined the photographs further. She returned with no clear answers, but pointed out that the mist was present in the negative and had nothing to do with the processing. The mist was part of the picture.

"That's really weird," was all her husband could say when she showed him the photos. What else was there to say?

A few days later, she picked up the other roll of film. When she got the photographs, she immediately took out the last four.

"The first picture was clear. The second was clear. You would think the third and fourth would be clear too. But in the third, two misty heads appeared. One is facing forward, and the other is turned to the side. I freaked out when I saw the picture. All I could think was that's two misty heads staring at me. I mean, you can really see all their features: nose, eyes, lips." Again, she asked the technician what she was looking at. Again, the girl had no clear answers.

When Cory returned home, she tried to show the picture to her husband, who simply dismissed it with a wave of his hand. He didn't even want to look at it. For more answers, Cory turned to a friend of hers in Calgary who worked at Kodak. She sent the negatives and received a phone call a couple of days later.

"That mist," her friend said, "is right in the picture. And it's not just any mist. Those are thousands of little dots, each a perfect circle."

Cory shook her head. She knew that nothing was wrong with the camera and that there had been no mist inside or outside her house when she took the photographs. She could only assume that the spirits of the recently deceased had decided to pay her a visit for the holidays, and their presence manifested itself in mists and vaporous heads. It was little comfort, to be sure.

And while her 11-year-old niece didn't like coming into the house and was terrified by the door that opened by itself and the accompanying phantom footsteps, Cory just took it all in stride. Her house had always seemed to be haunted. For years, she has heard people walking through the back door and up the two steps to the kitchen landing. Yet when she goes to greet her guest, there is no one there, and Cory realizes that she has just had a visit from an old friend.

"The incidents happened more often after the suicides," Cory says. "The house has always been haunted, I think. I believe its spirit has followed us from house to house."

For the uninitiated, an encounter can be quite harrowing.

Six months ago, Cory's sister spent two nights at her home while the sibling organized everything for her move into a new house. Cory was away on a trip for the two nights the sister needed the house, and after the first night she received a phone call from her sister.

The sister's voice was pinched and tense. She described coming over at 3 AM after work and heading off to bed. Cory's husband had already gone to sleep. A pharmaceutical technician, he was usually in bed by nine to prepare for his early mornings. But as she was in bed trying to sleep, Cory's sister heard someone open the back door. That was odd considering that she was sure she had locked the door when she came in. She heard footsteps on the kitchen landing and thought it must be one of Cory's foster sons coming home. Still, she thought it would be a good idea if she checked to see who it was. She found the back door shut and locked, the hallway deserted and dark. She called out names, but her voice just echoed back at her from the darkness. Had she heard the door open? Or had she imagined the entire episode?

Cory reassured her sister that what happened was far from unusual in her house. She had nothing to worry about; the spirit who liked to come in through the back door wouldn't harm anyone. For Cory's sister, the reassurances meant little. Spirits in the house? The idea alone was frightening, regardless of what the ghost's intentions might be. Still, she had nowhere else to stay and returned to the house again the next night after work. Again, she heard the same sounds. In the morning, she called her sister who again reassured her that she heard the noise all the time.

The experience made an impression on Cory's sister and she told her 11-year-old daughter all about what had happened. It might not have been the best thing to tell the little girl. When the three were on the couch in Cory's house, talking about what had been happening, they heard the back door open followed by footsteps. The conversation among them ceased.

"My niece's eyes grew wide as saucers," Cory says. "She looked at her mom and then at me and then started crying hysterically. Of course, no one was there."

As attuned to the spiritual realm as she is, Cory has no clue who the spirit or spirits might be. They might have something to do with the two young suicides but perhaps not. Regardless, her life, while unusual to most, is merely normal for Cory. Her mother and grandmother have had more than their share of paranormal experiences, so she's had help dealing with the frightening things that she sometimes sees and feels.

"Yes, it's hard," Cory says. "Sometimes, I've looked at people and have had horrible feelings about them. They don't frighten me. It's all just there and it always has been."

Thankfully, it's not all misfortune that Cory is able to sense. She laughs when she describes her gift for picking winners at bingo.

"I'll go to the bingo hall and predict who will win. I'll look at people, say, 'They'll win,' and they do," Cory says. "My girlfriends always say, 'Look at me, look at me! I want to win.' I have to explain to them that it doesn't work that way. I don't pick the winner. I just know who's going to win."

One evening, though, it happened. Cory looked at her friend and just knew something was going to happen. She grabbed a pen, and on the back of her card, wrote a name and a figure down. She folded the card and gave it to her friend with instructions not to read it until the night was over.

When the callers declared the night at an end, Cory's friend was flushed with victory. She had finally won at bingo, walking out with $2800 more than she had when she walked into the hall.

"Hey," Cory said. "Read the back of my card."

Her friend had forgotten about the card, but had put it in her pocket for safekeeping. She opened it, and there in Cory's handwriting was her name and the number 2800.

"I knew she was going to win money that night," Cory recalls, "and how much. I wrote it down and I was right."

Cory's gift works in many different and mysterious ways. But while some individuals would probably view her abilities as a curse, Cory takes it all in stride. After all, it's all she's ever known, and asking her to consider what a "normal" life would be like, with just the typical five senses, would be like asking someone to think about living blind, deaf or without taste or touch. You could imagine such a world, but would you want to? So it is with Cory, who feels she has been blessed with a sixth sense. While it can cause her distress, it has also opened her eyes and ears to a whole new world.

3
The
Maritimes

Grandma's Rocking Chair
FREDERICTON, NB

A common theme in Maritime legend and folklore is that inanimate objects, particularly those things to which a person seemed to have an extraordinary attachment, can sometimes become haunted or possessed by the spirits of those who have passed on to the "other world." Items such as mirrors, trunks, vases, photographs and walking sticks are among the most common things that are claimed to be possessed by their former owners. However, the most popular object often associated with a spirit is the rocking chair. In Nova Scotia, New Brunswick and Prince Edward Island, many stories are told about spirits that continue to be linked to their favourite rocking chairs long after their physical bodies have passed on. Nancy, a woman who resides in Fredericton, New Brunswick, tells one such story. She believes the spirit of her grandmother, who died some 15 years ago, continues to haunt the rocking chair she sat in for many, many years.

Nancy has fond memories from early childhood of the wooden rocker with its well-worn padded arms.

"I remember as a little girl going to visit my grandmother at her house and seeing her sitting there, rocking, in her favourite chair. Whenever I'd stay over at her house, I would hear her rocking late into the night, and whenever I had to get up to go downstairs to get a drink of water or to use the bathroom, I remember finding Grammy sitting there rocking, fully content in her chair. My earlier memories are of Grammy sitting there reading or knitting something for one of the young children. But as she got older and her eyesight got bad, she found it hard to see. But that didn't stop her from rocking. She'd sit there for hours, just rocking back and forth…back and forth."

About 15 years ago, after Nancy had grown up and moved out on her own to attend university, her grandmother passed away. Nancy points out that the elderly lady remained in her own home until her death and that one of her aunts had gone to live with her when failing health prevented her from being alone.

"She was fiercely independent, that old lady. You'd never convince her to move out of her house and into a nursing home. It just wasn't going to happen."

In the last few years of her life, Nancy's grandmother became very ill and required around-the-clock supervision, but her mind remained sharp until the day she died.

"You won't believe this, but she actually died sitting in that rocking chair. It was quick, they said. Her heart just gave up. My aunt went to the kitchen to make supper, and when she came back, she found Grammy slumped over in her favourite chair. She was dead."

Three days after Grammy's death, the family gathered at the stately home. On the night following the funeral, Nancy and several other family members stayed at the house with their aunt. Nancy planned to return to university to resume classes the next day.

"Counting my aunt, four of us were in the house that night. We were all sleeping upstairs."

Nancy admits that the day's events were emotional and difficult for the close-knit family. The grandmother had been the glue that kept them together, and everyone recognized

A young Fredericton girl noticed that her grandmother's beloved rocking chair continued to rock after she died.

the void that the old woman's death would leave in their lives. The four relatives retired for the night shortly after 11:00. The day's events had taken their toll, and they were exhausted. It didn't take Nancy long to fall asleep.

A few hours later, she says, around 2:30 AM, she suddenly awoke to a sound that she had grown accustomed to hearing over the years in her grandmother's house. It was the sound of the rocking chair in the living room downstairs where it had been stationed for as long as Nancy could remember.

She knew that no one had sat in that chair after her grandmother's death, but she assumed that one of the others in the house that night must have had difficulty sleeping and decided to go back downstairs. Someone must be rocking in her grandmother's chair, she concluded.

She lay in the bed for several minutes, remembering how she would listen to her grandmother rocking back and forth and how that sound would comfort her on those long nights when she had difficulty sleeping. After maybe 10 or 15 minutes, the rocking sound finally got to her, and she decided it was time to investigate, to see which of her relatives was awake.

Slowly making her way through the dimly lit upper hallway and then creeping down the stairs, Nancy got to the foot of the stairway where she could look directly into the living room and see the rocking chair. She had done this many times in the past, and when she was younger, she would find her grandmother sitting there rocking. Sometimes, her grandmother would beckon for her to join her, and when Nancy was really small, she would bounce into the room and climb up into her grandmother's lap where she would snuggle up to the older woman and fall asleep. The next morning, she'd find herself back upstairs in her own bed.

This night, however, only hours after the funeral, Grammy was not sitting in the chair. No one was sitting in the chair.

"The chair was rocking, all right, but it was empty. It was just rocking back and forth all on its own."

At first, Nancy admits, the sight of the empty rocking chair frightened her. "I think that would scare anyone."

But after watching the chair rock back and forth for several minutes, she began to feel a warm sensation sweep up over her body, the warmth embracing her much like her grandmother had snuggled her so many years ago. It was at that moment that Nancy realized her grandmother was once again in the place where she had always been so comfortable —her rocking chair.

Eventually, Nancy returned to her upstairs bedroom and closed the door. Climbing back into bed, she says she felt relaxed and at ease because she knew her grandmother had come home. Today, she is the proud owner of her grandmother's rocking chair, and she says that sometimes it feels as if her grandmother came with it.

"Sometimes when I'm around that chair I just feel warm and comfortable. It's like she's right there with me." Occasionally, even today, the chair will rock for several minutes, and at those times Nancy says she feels as though her grandmother has come for a visit.

The Club Has
a Ghostly Member
HALIFAX, NS

The Halifax Club was established in 1862 to provide a friendly, professional and private retreat for the exclusive pleasure of its members and their guests. Today, the club continues to serve as an important meeting place for business-minded men and women. It is a place where they can meet, toast the day's successes, dine or simply relax in a warm atmosphere of history and tradition.

And they just might also see a ghost because, according to local legend, the Halifax Club is haunted. Over the years it has been reported that the spirit of a well-dressed young man has been seen many times wandering the floors as if looking for something. What, however, remains a mystery, as does the man's identity.

Jason Clarke is the manager of the club located at 1682 Hollis Street in one of the oldest sections of Halifax. While he points out that he has never encountered the ghost firsthand, he has heard the stories that the ghost of a young man supposedly haunts the facility. And while no one knows for certain the true origin of the ghost, there are two possible scenarios for the hauntings.

The first revolves around one of his predecessors in the general manager's position, a man who worked there in the 1870s.

"He was one of club's first general managers. He apparently had some sort of emotional or mental issues, and things apparently got so bad that he eventually committed suicide at the club. It is said that he stabbed himself many times and then jumped out of the third-storey window. Sounds like a terrible way to go."

Is the ghost that reportedly roams the halls of the Halifax Club that of this troubled young man? Perhaps, but there is another possibility.

"Early in the 1900s, one of the members was at one of the local bordellos where he had a heart attack. The lady he was with supposedly phoned the club and told some of his fellow members what had happened."

Since the fellow was well known in the city, the members thought it would cause a scandal and ruin their comrade's reputation if it was revealed that he had died while in the company of such a woman. To protect their dead friend's image, the members of the club went to the brothel, gathered him up and took his body back to the club where they deposited him on the front steps to make it look like he was entering his beloved club when he had a heart attack and died.

It wasn't long after his death that patrons reported observing the mysterious young man wandering through the club. The chandelier in the formal dining room also began swinging in a way that it had not done previously. The downstairs cloakroom is reportedly another favourite haunting place for the alleged ghost. Jason says that they have had many reports of unusual phenomena in that location and of people saying they have "strange feelings" when they go inside.

Today, the Halifax Club remains one of the prime examples of the extraordinary history that surrounds the port city of Halifax—a building that apparently comes complete with its own ghosts.

He Hears Dead People
DEADMAN'S ISLAND, NS

The name says it all—Deadman's Island. No plaques, no crosses, no mounds, no monuments and no markings identify the graves of the dead. All that remain are two and a half acres of useless bog land surrounded by a spruce knoll.

In truth, Deadman's Island, on the mainland shore of the Northwest Arm thrusting out into Halifax Harbour, isn't even an island; it's a peninsula. But in this unhallowed ground, long since forgotten except in the storied annals of Nova Scotia history and local ghost stories, are remains of many French and American prisoners of war from the 19th century, who were taken captive by British regulars and Canadian colonial forces during the War of 1812.

At that time, Canada was still part of the British Empire, and Halifax served as the Royal Navy's most important base in North America. Historical records suggest more than 1800 American prisoners of war were held at a military detention camp on Melville Island, which is just 100 yards across the harbour from Deadman's Island. The prisoners were incarcerated there after being captured in spectacular sea engagements off the New England coast or in bloody land battles in the still unsettled wild areas of Upper Canada (now Ontario). When prisoners succumbed to either their wounds or to disease, they were wrapped in canvas shrouds, placed in rowboats and taken to a swampy area on Deadman's Island known as Target Hill. There, they were buried in shallow pits.

Although no precise American records from the era were kept, the British made it a point to note these deaths. These

Deaths of prisoners of war on Melville Island in the 19th century contribute to mysterious activity near burial sites on nearby Deadman's Island.

records reveal that 188 American servicemen are buried in the soggy ground of Deadman's Island. Unfortunately, there is no longer any way to identify the graves because the American servicemen are buried among an unknown number of French sailors and 104 African-American refugees, who had come up from Maryland during the War of 1812 and had died of typhoid, smallpox, pneumonia and tuberculosis. Later, Irish immigrants who died after they had fled the infamous potato famines were also buried there, as well as French and Spanish prisoners of the Napoleonic Wars.

With the then privately held land in danger of being sold to condominium developers, the people of Halifax purchased the property in the year 2000 in order to protect its special significance as a war grave and local historic site. In that same year, the American servicemen buried at Deadman's Island were finally honoured by their comrades in an official ceremony. Members of the 164th Civil Engineering Squadron, Memphis, Tennessee, Air National Guard were working with their Canadian colleagues on joint exercises in Nova Scotia when they learned of the gravesite. On June 23, 2000, they went to the site and installed 188 small American POW/MIA flags.

Over the years, Deadman's Island has been the subject of many local legends and ghost stories. Bones have come to the surface, graves have been unearthed by storms and people have stumbled upon human skulls. One story goes that in 1907, the owner of a local dance hall dug up three skulls from the swampy ground and installed them in his liquor cellar to frighten off thieves. Subsequently, the skulls themselves were spirited away.

Today, through a concerted effort of many dedicated volunteers and knowledgeable historians, Deadman's Island is recognized for its role in both Canadian and American history. But for many locals it remains a place of mystery. For Miguel Romero, a Nova Scotia psychic who has been researching haunted places in Canada and England for several years, Deadman's Island is the ideal place to hear spirits talk. Openly admitting that he hears dead people, Miguel is forthright and passionate about his special talent. When he insists that he can contact the spirits of those who have died, he does so with such conviction and sincerity that he dispels the doubt of even some ardent skeptics. Miguel says he acquired his unique gift at about eight years of age.

"I was a child. It was night, and I was in my bed. An apparition came to me and stood at the foot of my bed. It was natural that he came to me in the form of something a child would be comfortable with—a pirate. The figure was sort of transparent. I could see through it but the outlines were translucent and glowing. I was not afraid. It passed through me. It was like a jolt of energy had hit me."

After that encounter, Miguel says matter-of-factly, he could see things that other people couldn't see, but mostly he began hearing the voices of spirits. It didn't matter where he went or what he was doing, he says the voices came to him at any time.

Miguel grew up in Somerset, England. He eventually entered the British Special Forces and loyally served his country for 30 years. He came to Canada in 1999 and settled in Nova Scotia. During all that time, he says, the spirits have appeared to him.

"They seem to follow me no matter where I go. They come through to me. Sometimes they're solid; sometimes they're not. Sometimes I might not even recognize them as apparitions."

He is constantly haunted by the spirits. "I've heard my name called out loud in some rather inconvenient places such as shopping malls, for example. It's hard to respond when you're in a crowded place like that."

While some people would be frightened by such a talent, over the years Miguel has learned to accept his gift and has embraced it, turning it into a sixth sense. Today, he goes in search of spirits, visiting homes, cemeteries and other places where tragic events have occurred.

"You've got to convince people that you're authentic, there's no question about that, because some people have a problem accepting this sort of thing. But usually people who are bothered by spirits want me to come to their homes. When I go into a home, I say a prayer, and then I call upon the spirit that remains there by using a dousing or divining rod, which is nothing more than a metal coat hanger. I use it to discern the spirit's energy and to determine if it's a negative or positive spirit. I've run into both kinds. When I reach the spirit, I ask it if there is anything I can do to help and then I tell it that its work here in this world is done. If the homeowners are not happy with the spirit, I will move it along.

More often than not, the homeowner just wants to know who the spirit is and what it wants. But if the homeowner wants the spirit gone, I tell the spirit to move toward the light, that it has nothing left here to do."

Miguel knows that skeptics dismiss his work as "mumbojumbo" but he learned long ago to stop worrying about what others think.

"I know that many people out there have a difficult time accepting what I do because if they accept this, then they have to accept the possibility that other things may exist.

"That's hard for some people to do. I do believe in a higher power, but not in a biblical sense. I believe there's an energy that surrounds us, and I don't spend my time worrying about what others think of my work and me. I don't

know how they can knock something they don't know anything about, but there a lot of people who do just that."

Instead of dwelling on the naysayers, Miguel has gone
about his work with a belief that he has been given his gift for
a reason, and that could be to help spirits who have lost their
way. When investigating hauntings or going into places where
spirits may be present, Miguel uses specially designed audio
equipment to tape the messages he receives from the spirits.

He explains how it works: "If I tape these words spoken
by a normal person—'the moon will shine bright tonight'—
and play that back in reverse, it would be gibberish. But if I
play the same message through the spirit, it could come back
'Heather had a lovely car.'

"When a spirit speaks, it's usually quick and high-pitched.
Most people can't hear it but I can, and I tape the messages as
proof of what I'm hearing."

By taping these messages, Miguel can play them back
many times until he can speculate about the spirit's business
here on earth. He relates one incident where a spirit referred
to a trunk in its message. Subsequently, the homeowners
found an old trunk in their basement. It contained an item
the spirit wanted them to have.

"Spirits can become attached to a place or a thing, and
they may want us to do something with it. Sometimes they
can't rest until they get that message to us."

Miguel has had a variety of experiences with spirit messages. At one location, he heard a spirit say, "Don't do that to
Lucy!" He says the voice sounded as if it was almost singing
the message. When he played it backwards, the message said,
"Lucy went in an earthquake."

Conversely, some spirits are rude, he says. "In one message, it opens by saying 'Miguel, hello.' Then you hear a woman say something quite incoherent, yet when played back in reverse the woman says, 'Too much mimicking in here!' The male spirit then continues with quite obscene language."

While Miguel has investigated many haunted houses, he has also visited other places where spirits might dwell. Among them are the Halifax cemetery where many victims of the *Titanic* are buried, and Deadman's Island, one of his favourite places to find spirits.

"I had a mixed experience at the *Titanic* graves. I certainly heard a couple of voices, but nothing that jumped out at me. Deadman's Island was a different story. I heard many spirits speaking at that location—all men. They said a variety of things, such as 'Don't lose the kit bag' or 'No. No. No. Hats left on.' It was very distinct. Deadman's Island is a place with many stories to tell. It's a great place to hear the spirits speak."

He knows some people will never believe that he can hear the voices of dead people, but that doesn't deter him in his work. Today, Miguel uses his special gift to help people bothered by spirits and then to help them put the haunting behind them.

"I know many people will never believe in something they can't see or touch, but I know it's real. I know I hear dead people."

The Five Fishermen
and a Few Ghosts
HALIFAX, NS

Located in the historic section of Halifax, the Maritimes' busiest seaport, is one of the area's finest restaurants, the Five Fishermen.

While the menu features some of the tastiest food in the city, particularly its selection of seafood highlighted by succulent, fresh Atlantic lobster and a bottomless mussel bar, the establishment also serves up a healthy selection of ghost stories sure to whet the appetite of those with a hunger for the extraordinary.

The Five Fishermen at 1740 Argyle Street is known for the aggressive entities that are said to haunt its premises. The invisible presences are known primarily to haunt the building's second floor, and while patrons have not reported any incidents, the "spirit" or "spirits" have been known to harass the staff from time to time. The ghosts are said to push or trip staff members, whisper their names when they are alone in a darkened room, yell their names in the busy dining room and throw or move objects.

The building that houses the famed eatery has a long and interesting history. It is significant not only locally, but nationally as well. It was built in 1816 as the Church of England's National School. The primary aim of the staff was "the instruction of the poor, with particular attention to their religious and moral obligations." It was the first school in Canada where children could get an education for free, and the building is designated as a National Historic Site because it was the nation's first public school.

On the other side of the world, an English governess named Anna was living an adventure that would later fill the pages of a book called *Anna and the King of Siam*. This book inspired several movies, most notably the Academy Award–winning musical *The King and I*.

Upon leaving Siam (now Thailand), Anna Leonowens came to Halifax in 1876 where she established the first school of the arts in Canada. The Victoria College of Art was housed in the building now occupied by the Five Fishermen until January 3, 1884, when the name was changed to the Nova Scotia College of Art and Design and it was moved to a new location.

The building next housed the Snow and Company Funeral Home, which played important roles in two of history's most notable disasters—the sinking of the *Titanic* in 1912 and the Halifax Explosion on December 6, 1917. When the *Titanic* sank on April 14, 1912, during its maiden voyage to New York City from Southampton, England, about 1500 men, women and children lost their lives. The ship went down in the Atlantic about 640 kilometres south of Newfoundland and close enough to Nova Scotia that many ships were dispatched from Halifax to assist in the high-seas rescue attempt. Days later, some ships returned to port loaded with the dead. Many of the victims—mostly first-class passengers—were taken to Snow's funeral home.

Five and a half years later, at 9:05 AM on December 6, 1917, a munitions ship exploded in Halifax harbour. The largest human-caused explosion until the dropping of the bomb at Hiroshima in 1945, the blast killed 1900, left another 4000 injured and flattened two square kilometres of northern Halifax. In total, 1630 homes were completely destroyed and about 12,000 were damaged. Again, Snow's funeral home played an important role in the disaster, receiving many of the dead, who arrived by the truckload.

When Snow's abandoned the building in favour of larger, more modern facilities, it was then used as a warehouse until the winter of 1974, when it was renovated and opened as the Five Fishermen Restaurant. While its ambience and food keep the patrons returning, many believe it is the building's distinguished history that produces its unique atmosphere and perpetuates the many ghost stories associated with the structure.

Leonard Currie came to work at the Five Fishermen Restaurant 17 years ago. He believes it is only natural that ghosts would be found on the premises in light of the building's historic past and its connection to death. Over the years, Leonard has worked in various positions at the restaurant. He started in the kitchen on the day shift, then moved to the dining room. He has been a bartender, and today he is a server, primarily on the evening shift. It's a job he enjoys immensely, and he loves the building.

"It's wonderful working in a building that has so much character and has such a significant history," he enthuses.

That the building is known to be haunted doesn't bother Leonard all that much. He believes it adds to its character, and he has become the restaurant's official ghost expert. While he admits to witnessing many unusual happenings firsthand, he has also heard many stories from his colleagues.

"It seems like it mostly happens late at night or when the restaurant is closed for business," he explains. "It's not

While it served as a funeral home, the Five Fishermen received many of the dead from the cataclysmic Halifax Explosion.

unusual to hear footsteps coming up the stairs when you know you're alone.

"Glasses occasionally fly off the shelves, silverware and tables move and silverware falls off the tables onto the floor when no one is around. It's a little creepy, but it's not scary in any way. I don't know of anyone ever feeling threatened or anything like that. I think most people just accept that the ghosts are being mischievous when they do these things or they're just trying to get attention. The taps in the bathrooms and kitchen turn on by themselves, and sometimes when these things happen, people say they feel as though there's a presence in the room. Other people say they've heard voices calling out their names when there's no one else around."

Leonard himself says it's not unusual for one of the servers, including himself, to hear his or her name called out while they're in the middle of the busy dining room. "I swear I've heard my name called out. You think it's one of your customers, but when you check it out, you find it wasn't them."

He describes the voices as being clear and distinct so that it's easy to recognize his name when he hears it. "It's very clear. They say 'Leonard' as clear as you and I. One girl told of hearing someone whisper her name in her ear. She said it was so clear that she insisted someone was standing right beside her, but no one was there."

Leonard recalls his first experience with the spectre that haunts the building. "It was one day several years ago in the afternoon when I was setting up the salad bar. Supposedly, I was the only person in the restaurant. As I went about doing my work, I would bring everything from the kitchen, which is on the third floor, to the dining room on the second floor. I'd bring it all down on large trays. They were heavy, and one time when my hands were full, I heard a large crash from the dining area so I put the tray down and went to check things out. When I got there, I found an ashtray on the floor. I figured it had fallen off a shelf, but I didn't know how it could have. Things don't usually move about by themselves, unless they're in this place."

Instinctively, Leonard bent down to pick up the ashtray.

"When I stood up, I was facing a mirror on a wall. In the mirror I could see a man walking past a table just behind me. I was supposed to be alone. It was an elderly gentleman with long, white hair. He was sort of hunched over, and he was wearing some sort of long, outdated black overcoat. I thought I was the only person in the restaurant, so you can imagine my surprise. A few years ago, there used to be a man who would come by and collect food for Hope Cottage [a facility for the homeless]. I had seen him around in the past, but never in the dining room so it caught me off guard. At first I thought it was him, but I wasn't sure how he got in. Maybe the door wasn't locked after all, I thought. But it was."

Seeing the man in the mirror, Leonard quickly spun around to talk to him, but no one was there. When he turned back to the mirror, the reflection was gone.

"When it happened, I just dismissed it, thinking that maybe I only thought I had seen something but I really hadn't. I didn't talk about the incident for some time, maybe a few years."

Then Leonard heard the story of an incident involving one of the managers. "Like me, he was in the restaurant alone one afternoon. When the phone rang, he answered it. When he turned back around, he saw a gentleman standing in the front foyer. He told the man to wait, and that he would be right with him when he got off the phone. When he finished his conversation, he hung up the phone and turned back to talk with the gentleman, but the old man was nowhere to be found and the door was locked. No one could have come in. When I heard the story and how he described the older man, I knew it was the same man I had seen."

Admittedly, no one knows for sure who or what haunts the building that houses the Five Fishermen Restaurant, but many, including Leonard Currie, emphasize its connection with so much tragedy and think it is only natural that something extraordinary happens there. Do ghosts of the victims of the *Titanic* or the Halifax Explosion haunt the building? Or maybe Anna Leonowens herself pays a visit to her beloved school from time to time? Who can say for certain?

The Headless Ghost of the Isle of Haute
BERWICK, NS

Nestled in the centre of Nova Scotia's picturesque and fertile Annapolis Valley, the quaint town of Berwick rests strategically between North and South Mountains. Dating back to the early 1800s, Berwick has been at the heart of the province's lucrative apple industry and has commonly become known as the Apple Capital of Nova Scotia.

But while apples, and to a lesser degree other agricultural activities, have earned the historic town its rightful place in the province's economy, the community also has its fair share of ghosts and legends that have established its place in the annals of Nova Scotia folklore.

In the 1960s, Berwick became famous for sightings of a 20-foot tall humanoid creature covered in hair. For many years, stories of the legendary Parker Road Ghost, as it became known, spread far and wide as reported sightings of the mysterious creature grew in number. Those who saw the

According to Joan Balcom, a headless apparition protects hidden treasure on the Isle of Haute in the Bay of Fundy.

"ghost" reported a ghastly figure covered in fur from head to toe.

To hear witnesses tell of their encounters, one would assume that the creature was real. Eventually, however, the stories were debunked. It seems several young men in the community created the creature as a prank. They had no idea their creation would become the stuff of legend.

While Berwick resident, entrepreneur, historian and local storyteller Joan Balcom admits she knows little about the legend of the Parker Road Ghost, she is considered by many in her community to be an authority on other ghostly matters of the area, particularly those stories that surround the

Headless Ghost of the Isle of Haute. She is an author of two books, *Fundy Tales* and *Mystic East: More Fundy Tales*, which she sells in her gift shop, and one of her favourite legends is that of the Isle of Haute, an island situated just off the province's coast in the Bay of Fundy, about halfway between Nova Scotia and New Brunswick.

Not much more than a sandbar, the Isle of Haute is clearly visible from communities such as Harbourville and Margretsville. It is known locally as the "Rock in the Ocean" because on one end are tall cliffs estimated at 300 feet high. On the western tip of the island is a long sandbar and in the centre of that sandbar is a deep, freshwater lake that was once a favourite spot for the Aboriginal people who first used the land. Presently uninhabited, the island once boasted a manned lighthouse that guided ships into the ports located along the bay, but when a fire levelled it many years ago, it was never rebuilt. Today, a mechanical beacon leads the vessels safely to their berths.

A native of the Berwick area, Joan says she heard the stories of the headless ghost when she was a child. Throughout the years, she has maintained her interest in the legends, carefully documenting what she has heard about the island and the mysteries that envelop it.

In a voice that conveys her excitement for the story, she explains that there is a ghost that guards a treasure buried hundreds of years ago on the island by a pirate known as Captain Ned Lowe. The local fishermen usually avoid the island, particularly the area of the sandbar where the notorious pirate is said to have forced his crew to dig deep holes to bury his rich booty. The exploits of Captain Lowe are well known throughout Eastern Canada and it is speculated that the ruthless pirate may have accumulated a rich treasure of gold, jewels and other items of immense value. Today, however, despite countless excursions to the Isle of Haute, the treasure remains hidden and its value remains a mystery, guarded forever by a mysterious headless figure left behind by the bloodthirsty pirate.

According to the legend, once the crew had secured the treasure somewhere on the island, Captain Lowe beheaded one of his men and left him there to guard the treasure. It is believed that the ghost of this headless crewman walks the island to this day, protecting Captain Lowe's treasure and guarding the rock's best-kept secret. Over the years, many sightings have been reported of the headless ghost stalking the island's shores, and area fishermen do not allow themselves to be caught out near the island at dark. No one, Joan says, wants to be on or near the island on those nights when the fog comes in and the waters around the Isle of Haute grow calm. After all, when conditions are right, the Headless Ghost of the Isle of Haute is said to be the most visible.

Many people have reported seeing the Headless Ghost, but few are willing to talk about their experiences for fear of what others may think. One local fisherman, however, says that on a foggy night some 20 years ago, he was in the wheelhouse heading for shore when his boat passed near the island.

"I had heard stories of the headless ghost all my life, but I ain't never seen him before that night," he says. "Anyway, this night the fog was so thick I could hardly see the shore, and I guess I got a little too close to the island. By the time I realized where I was, it was almost too late. I nearly grounded her."

Quickly giving the wheel a hard turn, his boat immediately responded and the fisherman admits he narrowly missed running aground.

"It was a pretty close call, I'll tell ya that much—and in more ways than one."

As the boat skimmed near the island shore, he says he thought he saw something out of the corner of his eye.

"I knew there'd be nobody on the island at that time of night and under so much fog, but he was there, that's for sure. It happened pretty quick, but as I looked to the shore, I swear I saw him. He was standing there on the shore just awaitin' for me to land. He was big, and even though it was dark, I saw that he was wearing old-fashioned clothes. I ain't saying it was the headless ghost for certain, but I can tell you from where I stood, it sure looked like the feller didn't have no head. So you tell me. Was it a ghost or not?"

The fisherman admits that it was just a quick glance. As he navigated his vessel along the rocky coast, the fog quickly swallowed up the island until it was all but invisible.

"But I know it was him. It just gave me a creepy feeling when I saw him standing there. I kind of got cold all over. I knew whoever was on that island that night wasn't from this world. I could just feel it."

The Legend of Double Alex
SAMBRO ISLAND, NS

Standing guard at the outer entrance to Halifax Harbour, the Sambro Island Lighthouse, built in 1758 and first lit in 1760, is the oldest operational lighthouse in North America. The lighthouse stands on a granite island about two nautical miles outside the harbour's entrance, marking an area of dangerous shoals.

In 1749 Halifax was founded as the primary base for the British Navy in North America. The harbour, which has a wide entrance, a main harbour, a narrow channel and a large basin almost surrounded by land, is the second largest ice-free harbour in the world. Only Sydney Harbour in Australia is larger.

Halifax Harbour offered the British a safe haven for the largest fleet they could envision. The entrance, however, was often masked in fog, and the 30 shoals surrounding Sambro Island were a grave hazard. The lighthouse at Sambro Island was built and has since stood at the entrance, lighting the way for vessels carrying immigrants, war brides and refugees to a new land. It has watched the passage of fishing boats and the spreading sails of yachting fleets. For sailors, it is the last sight or sound of Halifax, or the first on a safe return.

In the 1930s, Sambro Lighthouse was designated a National Historic Site. It was destaffed in 1988 but is still maintained by the Canadian Coast Guard. In 1997, through the efforts of the Nova Scotia Lighthouse Preservation Society (NSLPS), Sambro was designated a protected heritage building. It is first on the list of Canadian lighthouses recommended for preservation by the Canadian Coast Guard to the International Association of Lighthouse Authorities.

In addition to its important place in Canadian history, the lighthouse at Sambro Island is believed to be occupied by a ghost locals know as Double Alex or Double Alec, depending upon one's vernacular.

Chris Mills, a former lightkeeper who is now involved in the preservation of lighthouse history, edits and produces the NSLPS journal, *The Lightkeeper*. Over the years, he has researched Sambro Island and the lighthouse, interviewing those who have lived and worked at the structure, most notably the lighthouse's principal keeper from 1964 to 1988, John Fairservice, his wife Marjorie, who was assistant keeper, and their daughter Kelly, who was the acting principal keeper at the time of the destaffing in 1988.

The ghost stories may actually have their origin in events that date back to 1833. Since 1796, men from the Royal Artillery had been sent to Sambro light to staff the signal station and to aid the king's ships as they entered and left Halifax Harbour. According to historical records, a set of signals consisted of one or two shots of a cannon fired at fixed intervals to alert vessels of the weather conditions inside and outside the harbour. By 1833, a small detachment of artillerymen manned the station with two 24-pound cannons. Historians believe that Alexander Alexander (Double Alex or Double Alec) was one of those artillerymen.

Chris Mills says that Double Alex has made his presence known many times over the years. John Fairservice reported strange occurrences on many occasions. A toilet mysteriously flushed by itself; a figure walked along the beach when the

Encounters with Double Alex, the spirit at Sambro Lighthouse, became commonplace for one lightkeeper and his family.

only other resident on the island, the assistant keeper, was asleep; and someone or something climbed into bed with one of Kelly's visiting friends.

Marjorie started hearing about Double Alex soon after the family moved to the island. "People used to come and visit, all the fishermen, and we'd hear all kinds of stories, but I was never nervous out there.

"There were lots of knocks on the door. One time, Johnnie was in having a shower and I was lying on the couch. I had Kelly sitting on me. We were playing and I heard those knocks, and I thought it was Johnnie fooling around. The knocks came again, and the next night we got word that my brother had died. If that was just a coincidence, I don't know.

"Sometimes you could hear somebody walking upstairs, and it wasn't our imagination. We had two dogs, and when they went to the foot of the stairs, the hair'd be standing up on their backs and they'd be growling, so they were hearing it too. But I've never seen anything."

John Fairservice recalls his first experience with the unexplained. "It was when Gasa Soltesz [head keeper in the early 1960s] was there. We went ashore, and we were on our way back. It was a nice calm day on the water, a beautiful day, and we seen this fella in a black outfit standing on the little beach by the thoroughfare. I asked Gasa who that would be, and he didn't know. There was no boats around, no nothing around. We docked the boat and went around that island three times and there was nothing there to be found, nothing to be seen there at all. Just up and disappeared, whatever it was, or whoever it was."

Both John and Marjorie recall hearing someone come to the house on many occasions, only they would never find anyone.

Marjorie says, "One evening we were sitting in the living room. We heard somebody come up the steps, come in and go down in the basement. We went to look, but nobody was there."

John adds, "Another time, we were sitting in the living room, and we had a porch on the living room entrance to the front of the house. It was never used, but the door opened and the door closed and the other little door coming to the living room opened and closed. We heard it. We were sitting there watching, and we didn't see the door open or close. Then we heard someone walk across the living room floor, go upstairs and into one bedroom. And we knew that Double Alec was in to visit us. And when he left, oh, I would say about a month or so later, you could hear footsteps coming across the floor, down the stairs and out through the porch as he left."

John also recalls the time a friend reported seeing Double Alex in their kitchen. "He came out one time to visit and he said he saw a guy sitting on a chair in our kitchen. He said, 'I can see him, John. He's sitting there.' And he described what he was wearing—a British uniform from the olden days—and he was telling me all what the guy looked like and everything. He said, 'Where did he come from?' And I said, 'I don't know, maybe he just joined us for a drink.'"

Another friend of the Fairservice family, a local fisherman, had his own experience with Double Alex. His story may hold a clue as to how Alexander Alexander became a ghost.

"Alec hanged himself. He was a soldier stationed on Sambro light. He went to a whorehouse in Ketch Harbour, spent another feller's money and back then, I guess that was quite the thing. So he hanged himself since he'd have ended up being shot anyway. He did it down in the shack on the shore. I got me a good scare from him one night. I'm telling you; it was something. They [the fisherman's buddies] were all tormenting me saying I was drinking.'"

The fisherman continues, "Well, we [he and his buddies] were out there carrying on, and they fired me overboard." It was a long walk from the shore to get to the house where the Fairservice family lived, but the fisherman made the trek in his wet clothes. Overhead ran a clothesline, which he notes is important to his story.

Once he got to the house, he removed his clothes, hung his blue jeans on the line and then went to bed.

"I got up at about two o'clock in the morning to get a drink of water. It was black, tick 'a fog blown' about 40. [It was a dark, stormy night with lots of thick fog and the wind was blowing at about 40 knots.] I just put the glass under the tap. I tried to be quiet because everbody's sleeping, when something hit the window. I dropped the glass and it was just like somebody blew it up into a million pieces. Glass shards was all over the sink, all over the counter, all over the floor. They [people who later heard his story] all laughed and went and said that it was the clothes on the line blowin' up against the window that scared the stuffing out of me.

"I went out the next morning and grabbed hold of that pair of pants and I came at the house with them and I stretched that line all it would stretch and it never came anywhere near the window. That gave me some scare." To this day, the fisherman is convinced it was Double Alex at the window that night.

According to Chris Mills, Minnie Smith grew up on Inner Sambro Island, one mile north of Sambro Island. One of 14 children, Minnie lived on the barren, windswept island until the mid-1920s. Hers was the last family to live on Inner Sambro, along with Ephram Smith, who tended the small beacon on the west point of the island. Minnie's grandfather, William Gilkie, was a lightkeeper on nearby Sambro Island, as was William's son Alfred and Alfred's son Arthur. In her later years, Minnie told Chris Mills another tale of Alex Alexander. Her story holds yet another clue as to how the ghost may have come to be.

According to the legend, a group of soldiers from England was camped on Sambro Island, and they had the big cannon guns out there. Alex went ashore with some of the other soldiers to a place known as Ketch Harbour or Duncan's Cove. They got drunk, and he was gone for a week. When he came back he was in pretty hard shape. He wanted the captain, the head fellow in the army, to give him a drink of rum to straighten him out. The captain wouldn't do it. So then Alex went and hanged himself in the whistle house.

Minnie picked up the story as she heard it. "I don't know who it was saw him [hanging there], but whoever it was came running down to my grandfather and said, 'Come quick. Alec hanged himself.'

"So the head fellow went up, and they cut him down. He was still warm and had a heartbeat. So my grandfather said, 'Do you have a penknife on you to draw out a little bit of blood? The veins will start going and his heart will come back.'

"The captain said, 'No, it's not allowed in the British Army.'

"So they let Alec die. He could have been saved, but they let him go. That's why I guess he haunted them. This was in my grandfather's time.

"Soon afterwards, the hauntings started. My grandfather had one of those big Newfoundland dogs. It was coming up a storm one night, and he said to my grandmother, 'Mary, I'll go check the boats, for it's going to be a storm.' And he went, and another guy came along. He took this dog along with him, and the dog wouldn't go ahead of him, just stopped right still.

"He called the dog, and the dog wouldn't go. When he looked, Alex was [standing] there but he never spoke. He was there for a minute or so, and then he just disappeared. That was the only time my grandfather saw him. But they heard noises and different things out there. Other people were supposed to have seen Alec on the island."

Today, the houses on Sambro Island are abandoned. If Double Alex still roams the island, no one is there to see or feel his presence. A few weeks before the last keepers left in March 1988, visitors staying overnight in the assistant keeper's house were awakened in the early hours of a stormy morning by the rustle of nautical charts being slid across the living room floor. No one was in the room at the time. Perhaps Alex was plotting a last fix on his position.

The Burning Ship
BAIE DES CHALEURS, NB

The burning ship of Baie des Chaleurs has both intrigued and mystified ghost hunters and onlookers for centuries. While there are many theories and explanations about the origins of the glowing fireball that turns into a three-masted schooner, no one really knows the true history of the phantom ship that plies the waters of Northumberland Strait between New Brunswick, Nova Scotia and Prince Edward Island.

Records reveal that the first sightings of the burning ship occurred in the early 1800s, when witnesses reported seeing a tiny flicker of light against the dark horizon. The glow gradually grows in intensity until it appears to burst into flames, outlining a three-masted ship fully engulfed by fire. Accounts of the fire's duration vary, but over the years it has been reported that the glowing ship can be seen for only a few minutes or for as long as an hour—until it seems to sink from view into the cold Atlantic Ocean.

One Prince Edward Island resident, Carol Livingston, has collected material and studied the legend of the mysterious burning ship of Baie des Chaleurs over the years. She has accumulated an impressive collection, and through her efforts Carol has learned that there are as many theories about the phantom ship's origins as there are sightings of the burning vessel. She has seen the ship herself on two occasions, once as a child and then again as an adult. Maybe her lifelong interest in the legend can be attributed to her early childhood encounter, but Carol says this story has fascinated her for many years.

Carol is a teacher who resides in West Point, Prince Edward Island, about 45 minutes west of Summerside. She tells many fascinating stories about the phantom ship that is seen mostly off the island's west point, at a place called Canoe Cove, and at the island's eastern point near Wood Island. The burning ship has also been seen from the coasts of Nova Scotia and New Brunswick.

"When I was a child, we lived close to the shore. From the upstairs windows of our house you could see the water clearly. When I was a little girl my father got us out of bed one night, telling us to go to the westerly windows and showing us the phantom ship.

"I was young and all I really remember seeing was a reddish glow out on the water, but he was certain it was the phantom ship. I always felt a little disappointed that my memory of that sighting was vague and indistinct when other people would talk about what they had seen."

That changed for Carol in 1987, when she and her two sisters were driving into Summerside on the Shore Road, Route #14, near the small seaside community of O'Leary.

"As we drove west, we passed through some trees. When we came out the other side of the grove, we looked out on the strait and could see lights out on the water. One of my sisters pointed out that it looked like the lights of New Brunswick were clear that night. That wasn't unusual. On clear nights, you could see the lights of New Brunswick from the island. Suddenly, we realized that the lights were much closer to the island side of the strait than New Brunswick, and we knew it couldn't be the lights from the other shore. Next, we concluded that it must be the lights of a passing ship. However, we quickly realized that couldn't be because it was still early spring and the strait was frozen solid, so no ships could get through. That's when it hit us. If it wasn't the lights from New Brunswick or the lights of a passing ship, then it must be something else."

Carol and her sisters reached the same conclusion at the same time. "We all chorused together that it must be the phantom ship. We quickly pulled the car over to get a good look. It was directly across from the west point near the west cape area. You could clearly see what appeared to be a ship, and it had two masts. Some people claim they've seen three masts, but that day we only saw two. It was close enough that you could see one of the masts was taller than the other, and the bottom part of the ship was on fire, as were the two masts. It was very clear and distinctive. Many people say they have seen crewmen climbing the rigging and jumping into the water and they say they hear people screaming, but we didn't see any of that. We watched it for maybe 10 or 15 minutes, then we had to leave as we were expected in Summerside."

Carol says they drove maybe a quarter mile down the road and then decided they'd stop to take one more look. By the time they pulled the car over to the side of the road and got out to look again, the mysterious burning ship was gone.

"It had vanished that quickly."

But Carol is sure of what she saw that day. "I know it was the burning ship. I'm positive."

Over the years, the mysterious flaming phantom ship has also been spotted near a place called Sea Cow Head. It has been seen in central PEI near Charlottetown and in the east from Wood Island to Murray Harbour. Carol's research has uncovered a variety of explanations for the phenomenon. Some people believe the burning ship is a form of St. Elmo's fire, moonlight reflecting off the water or glowing ink from a giant squid, although she admits she has difficulty accepting the last theory.

"I think I'd rather see a phantom ship or a ghost than a squid large enough to do something like that," she laughs.

Others theorize that the burning ship is an optical illusion, since the flames could be created from phosphorus on the water or gas emissions or some other type of natural chemical reaction.

Those who choose to believe in ghosts think that the mysterious ship is the *Barque Colburn*, which was lost near the coast during a violent October storm in 1838. Other possibilities include the *John Craig Light*, another lost ship that was smashed off the Shippagan Shoals in the 1800s; the *Isabella*, which sank in December 1868; the streamliner *Ferry Queen*, which went down in 1853; or an ill-fated immigrant ship bound for Québec. But Carol thinks the best explanation for the ghostly vessel's origins goes back hundreds of years and is connected to Portuguese explorers Gaspar and Miguel Corte-Real, who were said to have made voyages to the New World around the year 1500. Some believe Gaspar Corte-Real discovered Newfoundland before John Cabot and that historical records have him returning to Portugal with North American Indians for the slave trade. Gaspar's ship never returned to Portugal after a voyage to North America in 1501. When his brother Miguel set out to find him, he also disappeared. Both brothers were presumed lost at sea.

According to some legends, it is said that natives took the brothers by force, in retaliation for the men's actions and their brutality. Their ships were burned, and their crews were lost. Hundreds of years later, their ghosts continue to ride the waves of the Northumberland Strait in their ill-fated vessels.

Carol says she isn't sure what she saw that night when she was a child, but she is certain of what she and her sisters witnessed in March 1987. "I know what we saw. I have no doubts about that."

4
Newfoundland

Strange Happenings at the Long Point Light

TWILLINGATE, NL

Lighthouses are among the most visible and romanticized elements of Newfoundland's coastal architecture. They are magnets for tourists, hikers, photographers and nature lovers. They entice us with their size, their remoteness, their ruggedness and their history.

By the early 1880s, 33 lights were well spaced along two-thirds of the Newfoundland coast, stretching from Twillingate south around to Port aux Basques. Many would have you believe that a friendly spirit is associated with all lighthouses. Certainly many of the older ones have a strange story or two that no one can explain.

One person who knows a couple of these strange stories is Jack May. Mr. May is the lightkeeper at the Long Point Lighthouse, Twillingate, with its unsurpassed view of Notre Dame Bay. He started working part time at the light in 1980 and full time in 1988, after several years of working with the coast guard as a light station inspector.

The Long Point Lighthouse is the oldest lighthouse in Newfoundland that still has a lightkeeper. The lighthouse buildings were constructed in 1875 and the light was first lit in 1876. The lighthouse is interesting for its use of brick as a construction material. Brick was unusual for the time because the preferred building material for the most important sites was iron. A circular iron tower made up of metal plates bolted together was first tried at Cape Pine, at the entrance to Trepassey Bay, in the 1850s.

The lightkeeper's house at Long Point Light, Twillingate

In the old days, the power for the revolving gear that turned the light was supplied by a system of weights that hung down the tower, the same way weights are used to drive the mechanism of a clock.

Today the mechanism is driven by electricity, but the old system was used well into the 1950s because it was so accurate. Even when generators were brought in to provide electricity to the station, the lightkeepers opted to use the clockwork system, a system they were comfortable with and one that worked well most of the time.

The original clockwork parts are still at the Long Point Light, intact with the old weights and cables. Everything is still there, except for the big lens and the kerosene lamps, which have vanished over the years. Electric motors now do the work that would have been one of the lightkeeper's important chores—rewinding the weight apparatus every three or four hours during the time of operation.

Many years ago, sometime in the early 1900s, a light-keeper was working near the top of the tower. Although the old clockwork system was accurate, it still had some problems. The cables and weights sometimes got tangled as they went up the two levels of the lighthouse. When the cables knotted, the keeper had to take the weights off the cables wherever they were hung up, free the cable, put the weights back on and then restart the system.

Perhaps the keeper was engaged in some work like this at the top of the lighthouse shaft, just at the upper point where the lamps and the lens assembly are stored. He fell.

It was about 12 metres from where he was perched to the brick floor below. Nothing was there that he could grab onto as he tumbled down; the supports visible there today were not added until the 1980s.

The keeper certainly would have died or been critically injured were it not for a strange occurrence. Just before he would have hit the brick floor, he landed in the arms of a lady dressed all in white. When he turned back to thank her for saving his life, she had disappeared into thin air.

The story was handed down the line from one lightkeeper to another. The man swore he was caught, and to this day no one has any idea who the woman in white might have been or how an earthly woman could possibly have caught a full-grown man falling from such a height.

The Long Point Light is the site of another strange haunting, one that continues today. An old tar mop is kept at the base of the tower. The long-handled mop, with a round, brush-like head, was apparently designed for tarring roofs, but it was never used for that purpose.

When Mr. May arrived to work at the light, one of the lightkeepers who had been there for a long time told him that this tar mop had always been there. The tar mop rests on the bracket that supports the bottom part of the staircase. The reason it was never removed from the premises is that it has the strange tendency to move around all by itself.

According to reports, the mop is known to reverse its position on the bracket. One day it will be shoved in facing one way, and the next day, or two or three days later, it will be shoved in facing the opposite direction. There is no explanation for who does it, how it happens or why. It has a mind of its own and still keeps moving.

Certainly there seems to be something, or someone, at work in the Long Point Lighthouse. When asked if he had ever felt a friendly presence in the building, Mr. May responded without hesitating. "Oh, absolutely."

The One That Got Away
ARGENTIA, NL

Over the years, the Victoria Day holiday has spawned many stories. Many of them relate to camping trips interrupted by ill-timed snowfalls or to the great Newfoundland Victoria Day tradition of the first trouting expedition of the year.

What many may not know is that the holiday also has a unique ghost story.

The tradition of Victoria Day being a trouting holiday began sometime around 1900. Part of the reason for this is that by May 24, the ice has usually melted from most rivers and ponds. For the early part of the 20th century, the holiday was marked by the special railway run of the "Trouters' Special." The train left St. John's in the early morning, steaming for Argentia, a community southwest of St. John's where the ferry now arrives from Nova Scotia.

In May 1956, an author named Mark Ronayne wrote about the Trouters' Special. He wrote of "the joyful anticipation of knowing that all your friends will be on the train and that before five miles of clackety-clack go by every soul on the train will be your friend. Where else would one see so many stouthearted anglers at one time, such a variety of hats, rubbers (please don't call them waders) and clothing, of knapsacks, baskets and lanterns, of camps and kettles?" And while most of these holiday fisherfolk were busy swapping stories about legendary catches, some undoubtedly traded tales of the holiday's own phantom fisherman.

The tale of the Victoria Day ghost dates back to some time around 1920. One Victoria Day weekend, a man drowned in Gull Pond, near Windsor Lake, just outside of St. John's. The man had apparently waded out from shore in search of elusive trout, and he sank into a deep hole in the pond. His body was later recovered, but within a year rumours began to float around that the man's ghost haunted the pond.

In 1930, a St. John's man was fishing at the far end of Gull Pond. Finding himself without matches to light his cigarettes, he noticed another man fishing not far away. The second man was standing thigh deep in the water. The matchless man called out to the second man, asking him for a light. The second man acted as if he had not heard the question. Instead, he moved away and was eventually lost from sight.

At first, the fisherman thought little of the event, only cursing his bad luck for not having met someone more agreeable. It was not until much later that a friend told him of the ghostly fisherman who had been seen in that section of the pond.

In 1974, another encounter with the spirit was reported. An account of the meeting was later published in the *Newfoundland Herald TV Week*. On that occasion, three men spotted the ghost. It was getting dark when they noticed a man fishing off by himself at the head of the pond.

There was something unusual about the lone figure, so the three stouthearted anglers took a shortcut through the woods to get a better look. When they got closer, they saw that the solitary sportsman was a sad-featured man of about 30 years of age, and his face was ghostly white.

As the three watched, the figure of the man grew misty and faded into the deepening gloom.

The three men trudged back out of the woods. When they returned home, they took with them a story about the one that got away, a story which, that year, had nothing at all to do with fish.

The Victoria Day weekend remains, to this day, an important holiday for recreational fishing. While the train no longer runs, and propane stoves have replaced the campfires of old, it remains a holiday steeped in the fine traditions of yesteryear. Whether the ghost of the Victoria Day fisherman will continue to haunt Gull Pond remains to be seen. Next May long weekend, grab your fishing pole, head out to Gull Pond and see what you can catch.

The Jib-boom Ghost
ST. JOHN'S, NL

At the end of the 1800s, St. John's Harbourfront was a much different place than it is now. Foreign and local vessels filled the harbour, and the many piers clawing out into the harbour teemed with all varieties of merchants. Yet with the thousands of ships that passed through the Narrows at the entrance to the harbour, it is perhaps inevitable that the odd visitor from beyond the grave would join the living community of seamen and merchants.

Countless tales are told all around Newfoundland of ghost ships, galleons, warships, steamers and schooners of all sorts. A phantom Roman galley has even been reported in Placentia Bay, its decks and rigging aglow in unholy flames, the screams of its crew still audible after centuries of torment.

But it was in St. John's in the late 1800s that a very real ship became home to a most unwanted paranormal visitor. At that time, a particular schooner in the merchant trade was successful on all her voyages. The wealth and status of the captain and owner grew, and all was well for some time.

It was not long, however, before her luck turned, and no voyage prospered. No matter what business the ship was engaged in, the best efforts of captain and crew were fruitless.

The story of the jib-boom ghost in St. John's Harbour reflects maritime superstitions.

Every ship suffers small accidents, and every sailor makes mistakes, but this facet of shipboard existence seemed magnified on the cursed vessel. If anything could go wrong, it did. The number of accidents grew, goods were damaged in transport, items were lost mysteriously and profits dwindled on every journey. The crew, a superstitious lot to begin with, began muttering among themselves that some evil force had descended upon the vessel. The ship's reputation as cursed spread far and wide, and merchants were unlikely to charter her to carry their precious goods. Sailors feared to serve aboard her, and order on board the ship deteriorated. The captain was at a loss to explain the bad luck.

One night, the vessel was laid up in St. John's Harbour. The remaining crew was all ashore, leaving the captain alone in his cabin. Suddenly, and without warning, the cabin door opened. Much to the captain's horror, there entered from the darkness of the night the faintly luminescent figure of a man. Silently the man entered the room, and in the pale glow the captain could see that the figure had what looked like a rope around its ghastly neck.

The captain was surprised and greatly afraid. But as the master of the vessel, he bravely stood his ground and spoke to the spirit, saying, "In the name of all that is holy and righteous, who are you?"

To which the spectral form replied, "I am the man who hanged himself on the tree from which your jib-boom is made. While that remains on the ship, you will have no peace."

After speaking thus, the strange figure vanished.

The master of the afflicted vessel was a deeply religious man, and he was deeply troubled by the supernatural turn of events that evening. The next day he called in the ship's carpenter, who removed the spar from the cursed ship, constructed a new boom and fitted it into place. The captain bowed his head, said his prayers and waited.

With the removal of the jib-boom, it seemed that the curse on the ship was lifted. The daily routine of naval life returned and the flower of commerce blossomed once more. As far as I know, the ghost of the unhappy suicide was not seen again, at least not on that ship. Neither history nor local folklore tells us what happened to the infernal jib-boom itself!

The Harbour Grace Corpse Light

HARBOUR GRACE, NL

Mysterious lights have a great tradition in Newfoundland and Labrador. Stories from around the province tell of eerie lights that would appear in times of danger and were usually followed by a tragic incident.

Known in Latin as *ignis fatuus*, this pale flame has often been reported flickering over marshy ground and over churchyards. It often seems to appear in order to lead travellers astray, into bog holes or over cliffs.

The strange phenomenon is known most commonly in Newfoundland as the "jacky lantern," the West Country England name for the will-o'-the-wisp. It was also known as "corpse candle" around the capital city of St. John's and as "corpse light" in the picturesque, historic community of Harbour Grace.

One of Newfoundland's oldest outport communities, Harbour Grace has a rich and colourful history. As early as 1550, it was a thriving fishing community with the majority of fishermen arriving from the Channel Islands. In the early 1600s, fortifications were established at Harbour Grace by the famous English pirate Peter Easton, who plundered fishing stations, stole provisions and munitions, induced men to join his fleet and generally wrought havoc along the eastern coast of Newfoundland.

The community is no stranger to legends, and the corpse candle has a firm place in local folklore. In Harbour Grace, however, the strange lights were not always evil or dangerous,

After the mysterious lights of Harbour Grace led a man and his wife to this stone fence, the lost couple found a safe place to spend the night.

nor did they always lure travellers into treacherous areas. In one documented case, a corpse light actually led Reverend Canon Noel and his wife to safety during a blizzard.

That event took place at the beginning of the 20th century. The reverend and his wife had taken their horse and sleigh to a blacksmith several miles away. Delays meant the couple had to leave during a storm. Their horse soon became bogged down in high snow, and they realized they were completely lost.

A bright light began moving around. Believing it to be a sign of rescuers, the couple shouted for help. The light approached them and passed by, but no person carried it. The frozen pair walked in the direction of the light. It led them to a stone fence, which in turn led them to a house where they found shelter for the night.

When the two told the owners of the house of the strange light, they expressed no surprise. The corpse light was familiar to the citizens of Harbour Grace. It had been seen many times before, generally before some terrible tragedy. For whatever reason, the ghostly glow had decided to protect the reverend and his fair wife, instead of leading them to their doom.

Corpse candles were not restricted to land. In the early 20th century, a gentleman from the community of Shoe Cove Bight, near La Scie on Newfoundland's north coast, had a run-in with the ghostly light. This gentleman had seen a light coming in from the water. Thinking it was a boat coming in to land on the beach, he went down to meet it. He watched the light come in, but when it came close, its forward movement slowed. The light did not land on the beach at all. Instead, it chose to move parallel to the shore, as if it were a man with a lantern in his hand, walking on the water.

In spite of the widespread nature of the sightings, no entirely satisfactory explanation has ever traced the origin of these strange lights. One colourful Newfoundland folktale relates that the will-o'-the-wisp is named after a blacksmith named Will. Too evil for heaven, and with the devil unwilling to let him into hell, Will was doomed to wander for all time with only a burning wisp of paper to guide his way through the darkness.

It is generally believed in scientific circles that the flickering light results from the spontaneous combustion of gases, especially methane or phosphine, which is produced by the disintegration of dead plant or animal material and typical of the boggy terrain where the lights are commonly seen in Newfoundland. But whether it is bog gas, folktale heroes or wandering spirits, the corpse candle remains an intriguing part of Newfoundland's rich mythology.

The Ghost of Graveyard Cove
EMILY HARBOUR, NL

In 1949, a 15-year-old girl named Louise left Conception Bay to go up working "on the Labrador," the local phrase for the seasonal fishery that operated from the early summer to the fall by fishermen from Newfoundland. She set off with her father and three other men. Her father had a fishing room, a seasonal fishing station, in a little place called Tar Barrel in Emily Harbour, Labrador, five miles below Smoky on the way up to Nain. The "room" consisted of a house for the workers and a stage, the term for the raised, wharf-like platform with working tables, sheds and storehouses for fish and fishing gear. The girl cooked and worked in the stage, splitting and heading fish.

As she puts it, "Whatever a man could do, I'd do it."

While Louise and her father's crew worked on the Labrador, the fish was sold to J.W. Hiscock's in Brigus. A quintal (112 pounds or 51 kilograms) of dried fish would fetch between $4.50 and $5 if they were lucky. According to historian D.W. Prowse, Emily Harbour was a regular stop for the mail steamer, which ran between the first week of July and about the first week of November. Emily Harbour was also noteworthy as the final resting spot of the schooner *Shamrock* which belonged to the Rorke firm. That schooner burned in the harbour while loading fish.

Thirty crews plied the waters of the Emily Harbour area in the late '40s and early '50s, but Louise spent most of her first days there alone. Every morning she got up at 4 AM with the fishermen, served them breakfast and then made bread, scrubbed clothes with the washboard and did other chores while the men were out fishing. They would return around 1:00 or 2:00, which left her alone for the better part of the day.

Instead of roads between the different fishing rooms, there were rabbit paths that added to the sense of isolation. The girl's brother and one of the other fellows used the isolation, combined with the 15-year-old girl's newness to Labrador, to tease her and to make her even more nervous than she was already.

"Now Louise, if you see a bear come ashore, go into the porch and throw the whole hundred pounds of beef out," they told her. That way she could run away and let the bear eat the beef, instead of her. Louise was so afraid to be alone that she would get up out of her bed and crawl into her father's after everyone had left.

Every morning when the men went off fishing, Louise would take out her father's 12-gauge shotgun. She did not know how much powder to use, so she poured in a generous helping, a bit of wadding and a bunch of shot. With the

While working at Emily Harbour, a young woman kept hearing the ghostly voice of an unidentified little girl.

loaded gun beside her, she felt much safer. Then each day before the men came back, she would go down on the stage-head, pull the trigger and let the sound of the gunshot roar out over the water.

As cook for the room, one of Louise's jobs was to make bread every day. To do this, she used 100 pounds of flour a week. Around 7:30 AM, after she had made the bread for the day, she would go down to the stage to jig for fish.

One day, after she had been there about a week, she went down on the stage and heard a voice say, clear as day, "When are you going home?"

Now the girl thought she was alone, but she looked around to see if someone had come up behind her. She could see no one.

The next day she went back out on the stagehead. Once more, the same as the day before, the unseen person called out, "When are you going home?"

The girl thought, *I have to find out about this.*

Off she went exploring. It was not long before she walked down into one of the nicest looking places she had ever laid her eyes on. It was a little gulch with a beautiful sand beach and hills on both sides. Not more than 50 feet back from the beach were three grave markers. But try as she might, Louise could not read what was on the headstones because they were too weathered. She gently straightened the old headstones and headed back to the house.

Later her father told her that years before, back in the 1800s, a family had died in Emily Harbour of smallpox, and that the family had to be buried on the Labrador. The little gulch that she had discovered was named "Graveyard Cove." Up to this point, the girl had been scared, but she was not scared when she learned the story. She returned to Graveyard Cove and placed wildflowers on the three old graves. The ghostly voices stopped, and the girl returned with flowers every day until the end of the summer when she sailed back home to Conception Bay.

Several years later in the 1950s, Louise was back in Emily Harbour but living in a different room because she was married. She went down again to the stage one morning. This time, she heard a baby crying. She had two children by this time, but the crying was not coming from either of them.

The sound was coming from a distance away, up on the back of the hill. She thought that there had to be someone living up there, so once more she set off in exploration. She found no one there.

For two or three days in a row, she heard the baby crying. Finally, she asked some of the older people about the phantom baby and its cries. They told her that many years before, a woman in the community had given birth to a baby that had died in infancy. The grieving mother had buried it up on the back of the hill. Louise looked for the grave but was never able to find it. Local legend told that she was not the only one to have heard the unearthly cries, and that they were a common sound in the air of Emily Harbour.

Today, the entire community of Emily Harbour is a ghost of its former self. What was once a bustling collection of fishing rooms is now a quiet place, its days of business and community life long faded. Its stories, however, live on.

5
British
Columbia

Music in the Walls
AGASSIZ, BC

Moving to the country to get away from it all—that's half the attraction of living in the small community of Agassiz. Located in the heart of the stunning Upper Fraser Valley, the historical town has its roots in the region's first explorers and inhabitants. In the early 1800s, settlers began to farm the fertile lowlands, and the quest for gold in the late 1850s drew thousands more to the area. The trend to settle in Agassiz continues even now, but one family got more than it bargained for when deciding to take up residence in the valley. Their old farmhouse came with an extra bit of history and possibly the spiritual remains of some previous resident.

The couple, whom we will call Jane and David, shared their story with an online newsletter about haunted places. Only two or three weeks after moving into the old, remodelled farmhouse, "things started happening."

The couple was in bed when a loud crash startled them. "It sounded as if someone had dropped a load of lumber at the end of our bed." Alarmed, David checked all over the house, both inside and out, but could find nothing wrong nor any source for such a loud noise.

As weeks turned into months, more things happened. First, the couple could hear music playing in the living room where a wood stove used to be. It wasn't modern music, as if they were hearing someone's radio, but old-fashioned music. It sounded almost as if the tunes were coming from somewhere inside the living room wall.

Then came the more tangible signs that something other-worldly was part of the bargain when they bought the house.

"One afternoon, we both saw what looked to be a smoky mist form in mid-air and then dissolve," says Jane.

They kept secret the notion of a ghost in the house, but people coming to stay picked up on the unusual goings-on. After an overnight stay, guests would ask the next day, "Did you have a radio on at night?" or "I woke up to music playing." Some guests claimed they felt something touch their legs during the night, and it scared them so much they refused to stay there again. One guest heard glass smashing and what sounded like the basement door being dragged open and pushed shut.

After two years with the farmhouse ghost, David and Jane finally moved. They know that the house is still standing and Jane is curious. "I don't know if the new people have had this sort of thing happen to them. I sure do feel like asking them!"

Brady and His Lady—
Ghosts at the Bedford Regency
VICTORIA, BC

The spacious lobby of the elegant Bedford Regency Hotel in Victoria is warm and welcoming. Many guests enter the historic hotel, with its vaulted ceiling, wood panelling and chic furnishings, charmed by the surroundings and completely unaware of its colourful past or its unusual current situation. There are ghosts at the Bedford Regency, and even if you don't see them, a whiff of cigar smoke or strong cologne will inform you of their presence.

The hotel, which sits in Bastion Square between Government and Langley Streets, is the original Hibben-Bone building, named after Thomas Hibben and William Bone. Hibben was an American entrepreneur who moved to Victoria during the 1858 gold rush in hopes of striking it rich. Instead of panning for gold, he set up a bookstore and stationery business and made his fortune in a more traditional manner. When Hibben died in 1890, he left his business in the hands of his wife and two sons but managed by long-time employees William Bone and C.W. Kammerer. Hibben's business burned to the ground in 1910, but out of the ashes rose a magnificent new structure—the current home of the Bedford Regency. The new Hibben-Bone building housed various professional offices as well as the bookshop, but eventually the building's owners fell on hard times.

Beds replaced books when the Churchill Hotel opened in the mid-1950s; however, the hotel did not live up to its auspicious name. Historian John Adams writes that the Churchill's basement-level beer parlour became a well-known rendezvous point for those prowling the seamier side of life. Prostitutes, drug users and criminals drank until dawn in the smoky, dimly lit pub, and the hotel rooms were used by guests who tended to pay by the hour. In the 1980s, Sam Bawlf rescued the building from its fate and restored it to be an upper-class hotel called the Alhambra. Shortly after, it changed hands again and was renamed the Bedford Regency.

It didn't take long for the staff to realize that the hotel was haunted. Housekeeper Lucy—who prefers we use only her first name—joined the Bedford Regency in the early 1990s. She first met the hotel's ghost down in the rather creepy basement beer parlour. Because the hotel is built on a hill, the basement bar is at the back of the building with stairs that lead up to street level.

When I visited the space, I found a dark, dusty area with remnants of the old pub, such as the counter area, still in place. Much of the interior has been torn out, and it looks like a construction site. Since it isn't used for much else these days, many of the employees go down there for their lunch or coffee breaks. Lucy told me that when the hotel was being renovated, she had gone down to tidy up after the construction workers who used the area for their lunches.

Lucy remembers, "I saw the shadow of a man wearing a derby hat walking down the stairs that come in from outside. I was sure the door was locked so I commented that someone must have left the door open."

One of the construction workers who was with her said, "Oh, that's just Brady." The workers told Lucy that Brady was the resident ghost, but she thought they were joking.

"I got up and took a peek up the stairs but no one was there. Then the shadow moved down the wall, and I could feel the energy. I smelled a strong men's cologne and cigar smoke."

The door at the top of the stairs was locked. Lucy realized she had encountered her first bona fide ghost. It wouldn't be her last encounter, though.

Up on the fourth floor of the Bedford Regency, in room 49 overlooking the harbour, the ghost of a former female guest has taken up permanent residence. The scent of her perfume can be so strong that one hotel guest actually accused her partner of entertaining a woman in their room while she was out. Lucy laughs, saying the ghostly woman—whom employees have nicknamed Lady Churchill—likes to lock and unlock the doors to room 49.

"I have also felt someone brush past me while I'm cleaning in there. One gentleman asked me if I had seen anything. He saw a woman in a yellowish gown with ribbons and a hat, and he smelled perfume."

In an interesting twist, it turns out that Brady, the cigar-smoking ghost in the bar, was having a relationship with Lady Churchill. Brady was one of the regulars at the bar, which is how he met his ladylove. One day, he came down the stairs looking for his girlfriend, only to meet another man at the bottom of the stairs with the same intention. A fight ensued, and the other man fatally stabbed Brady, who died in a pool of blood on the stairs. Local lore says that Lady Churchill may have died of a drug overdose in her room—a collection of drug paraphernalia apparently found in the room during renovations supports that theory.

Guests often report seeing or smelling the hotel ghosts. In 2002, Lucy recalls that one man staying in room 49 came out and asked her, "Can you stop that man?" No man was in the hall, and no one had passed her. The guest could have sworn he'd seen someone leave his room. Could it be that Brady had wandered up for a visit with Lady Churchill? Another guest claimed to have woken in the middle of the night to see someone standing at the foot of the bed. To the guest's astonishment, the apparition turned, and without a word walked through the wall.

Recently, when another pair of hotel guests came down to check out, they asked if spirits were known to be in the building. They were asking because they had a powerful feeling of negativity that overwhelmed them when they walked in the hotel. They knew nothing of Brady or his lady before coming to the hotel.

Lucy says that Brady shows up fairly regularly, and he likes to play games with the elevator or with the lights and door locks. "He freaked me out one day, stopping the elevator seven times in one shift." But for the most part, Brady sticks to the bar.

Lucy's most recent personal encounter also frightened another of the housekeeping staff. "Some of the housekeepers were down in the basement area on a break. One of the girls put a book on the old bar counter. It flew off the counter and landed on the floor." The woman accused Lucy of knocking her book onto the floor, but Lucy was three feet away. "I said that I didn't touch it!" That upset the other housekeeper, who didn't know until that moment that her workplace had a ghost.

Brady also likes to play tricks on Bob, the maintenance man. "He locks doors in a way no human could," Bob says. "I'm a spiritual person, though I didn't really believe in ghosts until I worked here. Now, after six years, I realize there's more to this place than meets the eye.

"The last one for me was in the summer of 2002. A staff member reported that one of the vacant rooms was locked from the inside. I figured that someone must have left a window open and that the door slammed shut, jarring the deadbolt slightly so that it locked the door." Bob tried to get the door off its hinges but it wouldn't budge, so he had to get a ladder and crawl in through the window. The window, he noted, was closed. When he got to the door, he saw that the deadbolt was fully turned and locked. "I'm the only one with a key for the deadbolts, and I didn't lock it." The room was empty and immaculate. "Whoever locked it didn't leave by the door or the window."

Both Bob and Lucy have their ways of dealing with the ghosts. "When Brady comes around," Lucy says, "I just stamp my foot and tell him, 'Brady, go away!' " About a year and a half ago, she discovered this tactic seems to get him to leave and stop playing tricks. Bob talks to the spirits, imploring, "Look, let me just get this done."

On my tour of the hotel, I didn't notice the negative energy that guests reported. However, for what it's worth, when Lucy showed me the section of the bar where the book had flown off the counter, I did feel a distinct prickly feeling, as if I was standing next to one of those static electricity balls at a science centre. And the hair on the back of my neck stood on end. Was that the power of suggestion, or did Brady greet me as only a ghost can?

O'Keefe Ranch

VERNON, BC

Nestled in the scenic, rolling hills of the Okanagan Valley near Vernon, the O'Keefe Ranch houses more than just a wealth of local memorabilia. The ranch also keeps a few ghosts on hand to augment its status as a well-known tourist attraction. The paranormal here prickles the senses, from an unexpected chill in an otherwise warm room to a disturbing sense that someone else is present and watching.

There may be some valuable clues in the ranch's history about whose spirit resides in the rural micro-community. Cornelius O'Keefe founded the cattle ranch in 1867. It was a time that many now might find hard to imagine, when the land stretched unfenced from the U.S. border to the Shuswap. Thousands of cattle grazed on the lush bunchgrass ranges and sheltered near the cool upland forests of the Okanagan Valley. A handful of ranchers held most of the land, and Cornelius O'Keefe was among them. He started with 160 acres, the maximum allowed by the colonial government, and over the years his empire grew as O'Keefe acquired unoccupied crown land for as little as a dollar an acre.

In its earliest days, the ranch was at the end of the wagon road into the Okanagan Valley. From its humble beginnings, the O'Keefe family built up a small settlement consisting of a general store with the first post office in the Okanagan, a blacksmith shop, St. Anne's Church (in which weddings are still held) and many other buildings. O'Keefe also built a beautiful Victorian-style mansion for his wife, Elizabeth, so that she could enjoy ranching life in comfort.

St. Anne's Church is one of several historic structures erected by the O'Keefe family.

By the turn of the century, the O'Keefe Ranch had grown to cover more than 12,000 acres. But the end was near for the great ranches of the Okanagan. The orchard industry moved in, and the pressure to sell was great as thousands of would-be orchardists arrived on the newly completed railways. One by one, the huge cattle ranches were sold off. Cornelius O'Keefe was one of the last to sell. In 1907 he sold to the Land and Agricultural Company of Canada, which subdivided the ranch into orchard land. But the O'Keefe family stayed, continuing to ranch on a smaller scale and living in the beautiful mansion that O'Keefe had built during the ranch's heyday.

After Cornelius' death in 1919, Elizabeth, and later his son Tierney, managed the O'Keefe Ranch and carefully maintained the buildings and grounds of the original ranch "home site." It was Tierney O'Keefe and his wife, Betty, who opened the ranch as a heritage site in the mid-1960s. They restored the remaining buildings, relocated the blacksmith shop from its original location down the road and reconstructed the general store. In June 1967, 100 years after its founding, Premier W.A.C. Bennett opened the ranch to the public, ushering in a new era for this historic place. The property eventually came to be owned by the City of Vernon, and a nonprofit society now operates the business.

The O'Keefe House, with its magnificent interior filled with the family's priceless Meissen porcelain and silverware, seems to be the building where some visitors have unusual encounters. Various people have seen a lady in white peering out of the upstairs window and then disappearing moments later. Also, staff at O'Keefe Ranch have said that, when they are in the mansion alone at night, they sense a woman walking past them in the hall. Visitors have also reported walking into distinct cold spots—thought by most paranormal experts to indicate an otherworldly presence. Others report getting an eerie feeling when they enter the building. Tour guides often get feedback from some members of their groups that they could sense something unusual.

"The people who lived here have definitely left behind impressions," says the current curator, who has lived at the mansion for 19 years and prefers not to be named. "Much like the wallpaper on the walls, the impressions are faded but still give a sense of the personalities, especially the stronger

Visitors have reported a variety of paranormal phenomena in the family's former home.

ones. We had a former office manager who always said she could sense the people without needing to see them."

The house also includes, among its treasures, a turn-of-the-century rocking chair, which has been seen by visitors and staff to move without anyone sitting in it or touching it. Many reports also exist of people feeling as if someone or something is watching them when they are in the kitchen.

One night, a groundskeeper who was making his rounds saw the curtains in one of the mansion windows move as though someone was standing behind them and peering out.

He raced into the house to chase what he thought were probably mischievous kids playing inside after hours. However, when he got inside, he found the house was empty and the curtain was hanging normally.

Could Elizabeth and Cornelius still be watching over their beloved property? That seems to be a reasonable conclusion, given that the O'Keefes were the sole occupants for more than 90 years, and the family was buried on the property in the graveyard behind St. Anne's Church. However, the current curator told me there is another possibility.

"The woman's presence seems consistent with a governess who lived here," he says. In addition to feeling a woman's energy, some guests who are sensitive to the spirit world claim to have glimpsed a female ghost in the former governess' room. The curator says there have also been reports of the governess' door mysteriously unlocking on its own.

How is it that a former employee remains so tied to the old homestead?

"Well, we do know that Cornelius was a randy old fellow," says the curator. The records speak for themselves. Mr. O'Keefe had two children by a Native common-law wife and nine children by his first white wife, Mary Anne. After Mary Anne's death at age 63, Cornelius married 23-year-old Elizabeth and sired six more children. His last child, Eileen, was born when he was 76 years old, hence the need for a live-in governess.

"Rumours abound of his dalliances, and it is possible that Mr. O'Keefe had a relationship with one of the governesses," explains the curator. "I live in the back of the house by the kitchen, and recently I've had a strong sense of Cornelius and the governess. I don't know why but I just picked up on the idea that something happened between them."

Perhaps O'Keefe Ranch is populated less by ghosts and more by the pervasive and persistent energy that this pioneer family created in their near-century of living there.

Phantom of the Burn Unit
VANCOUVER, BC

A good bedside manner is always welcome when you're stuck in a hospital bed. But what if the caring attention comes from a spectral helper? Another spine-tingling story that lends new meaning to the marketing slogan "Super Natural British Columbia" comes from veteran employees of Vancouver General Hospital's Burn Unit.

A young man named Douglas was terribly burned along with 16 others in an explosion at a Vancouver grain elevator in the mid-1970s. Douglas apparently suffered greatly from his burns, but he seemed to be making progress. Such courage and dogged will to live garnered both the respect and favour of the ward nurses who attended to the plucky man in room 415. Suddenly, despite his improvement, he announced to a nurse on duty that he was very tired. Soon after that, Douglas died.

Not long after Douglas' death, his former room and the burn ward became a kind of eerie show-and-tell. There were stories of toilets flushing and radios turning on when no one was near. Nurses reported seeing vague shapes moving around Douglas' empty bed. An orderly claimed to see bedsheets being turned down, as if to make the bed ready for someone. However, the apparition wished to be even more helpful.

Many in the ward said they witnessed a ghost comforting some of the more seriously ill patients. In one instance, a critically burned woman told the staff of a young man who had visited her on the ward. This surprised the attendant nurse, since no one outside patients' families were permitted on the floor.

When asked who the visitor was, the patient replied, "He said his name was Douglas."

The ghost of Douglas was apparently active until the burn unit was torn down. There have been no recent sightings of the soothing spirit in the hospital's new site.

Sabrina's Surrey Spectre
SURREY, BC

When we lose one sense, all our other senses become enhanced, but does that include the sixth sense? For a young blind girl in Surrey, that seems to be the case. Ten-year-old Sabrina saw a ghost in her family's home, and her mother, Colleen, says they now fear that the spirit of a dead jogger haunts their dream home.

For the purposes of this story, the family will be the "Albright" family. When the Albrights moved into the stylish, three-storey house in the Newton region of Surrey, Colleen says they had no reason to suspect that anything could be spiritually amiss. It was a brand new home, and they were the first owners. The houses were constructed on what had been an open field, so even the energy of previous residences couldn't have carried forward.

Colleen knew a lot about that sort of thing because she and her family had lived through some odd, inexplicable situations in their previous home. In the mid-1990s, the Albrights experienced paranormal phenomena in another Surrey home.

"I always thought something was weird in that house, too," says Colleen. "It sounds bizarre, but our hydro bills would be high to the point of being ridiculous."

Though the Albrights had only one small child and were out during the day working, they received staggering heating bills of $500 to $600 every two months. Sabrina was about two years old at the time, and Colleen says her daughter used to become agitated at night and refuse to sleep in her room.

"She would point to the electrical panel box in her room and say, 'Baby! Baby!' But we never knew what that meant." Accounts exist of people who have seen entities emerge from electrical outlets, but none of the other Albrights had seen anything of the sort.

Their plight attracted the attention of television producers from a show about paranormal experiences. "But even they had trouble," says Colleen. "They couldn't even film there because the camera batteries would suddenly be drained." Although they suspected that something or someone was stealing energy from the house, the Albrights could never prove it.

In 1999, the Albrights moved to the big, sprawling house that was their dream home. By now they had a son, Brandon, and Sabrina's vision was deteriorating. At the age of six, Sabrina was diagnosed with Stargardt disease, a rare form of macular degeneration that impairs a person's central vision while leaving the peripheral vision intact. Within six months, Sabrina's vision sank past 20/200 (legal blindness) to 20/400. And while she still had her peripheral vision, the little girl lost her ability to see colour. Stargardt disease affects the centre of the retina, which is responsible for the fine, detailed central vision (used in reading) and colour vision.

"It's been four years," says Colleen. "Sabrina manages quite well now with her peripheral vision. She skates and skis. She doesn't walk into walls."

But in late February 2003 something happened that both frightened and enraged Sabrina's mom. "I am more scared of this than she is," Colleen explains. "I was mad. Why would they want to scare a little blind girl?"

That day the family routine of getting the kids up, dressed and off to school was under way. It was about 7:30 AM, and Sabrina was already dressed. She was in the hallway, waiting for her six-year-old brother, who was using the toilet in his parents' ensuite bathroom. Colleen went downstairs to the kitchen to have her morning cup of tea.

"When I went down, Sabrina was in the hallway looking into our room. When I came up, I found her protecting Brandon while he was on the toilet," remembers Colleen. Sabrina looked deeply relieved to see her mother. "She said, 'Oh, mommy, I'm so glad you're here. There's someone in your room!'"

Colleen didn't see anyone in her large master bedroom, but Sabrina insisted. Her obvious state of alarm convinced Colleen that her daughter was serious.

Colleen says, "She told me that she saw someone walk from one end of the room to the other." At first, the person appeared to be solid, which prompted Sabrina to rush to stand between the stranger and her little brother. "But then she saw the person walk through the dresser."

According to Sabrina, the ghost is a woman. "She said that if it's a man, he wears girl's clothes." Sabrina couldn't make out the face, but she did supply amazing detail. She saw a tall, skinny person with blond hair wearing white running shoes, white socks, a white short-sleeved shirt and blue and green multicoloured jogging shorts.

Colleen reminds me, "She's also colour blind, but somehow she saw the colour." It was Sabrina's attention to detail and obvious fear for her brother's safety that persuaded her mother that her description wasn't a daydream or childish prank. "Sabrina was adamant that the person had pink skin, which she could see because she wore a short-sleeved running shirt and shorts."

The mysterious "person" didn't turn to look at Sabrina. The phantom just walked through the room and disappeared. That upset the little girl. She told her mother, "She didn't even say hello."

Colleen knows that whatever Sabrina saw, it wasn't a real person. "I don't know what it was."

The day before Sabrina's ghost sighting, Colleen had a feeling that she wasn't alone. "I was in bed, and I had a really weird feeling that someone was watching me." She was already feeling spooked because her dial-up Internet had connected that day "without me dialling." She picked up the phone to hear the hiss associated with a computer modem. "It took me a while to get the modem to shut off so that I could use my phone. At the time I didn't think much of it, but now I wonder."

The Albrights don't talk about the ghost sighting much now, preferring not to make more of it than it was. "But since then I am more aware," says Colleen. "The house creaks a lot because it's new and it's settling. Now and then I get a weird feeling."

Sabrina doesn't talk about the ghost either. She's already more preoccupied with school and her friends. Her mom still harbours some anger at having her dream home invaded by an uninvited entity.

"I'm so mad because I don't want any of these things. I've seen UFOs and have gotten over it, but enough is enough."

Colleen is curious about the nature of the spirit. She wonders if there had been some violence in the area before the houses were built. She plans to ask around to see if her neighbours know of anything. "Maybe a jogger was killed here, who knows?"

Or could it be that the Albrights brought the otherworldly energy with them when they moved?

The Alibi Room
VANCOUVER, BC

Maybe it's the banging about or the frantically swinging bathroom doors, but the ghost at the Alibi Room in Vancouver's Gastown district seems to be upset about something.

Most of the staff have had run-ins with the resident ghost. Head bartender Jeff Breeken told a *Vancouver Sun* reporter, "He scares the death out of me."

For reasons unknown, the spirit at the Alibi Room in Vancouver likes to shake the washroom door.

Breeken claims he is not easily frightened, but even his macho demeanour withers when the ghost makes its presence known. "It's pretty freaky. One night I went downstairs and heard all this banging. I thought it was the trains outside making the noise. I look out, and there were no trains."

In 2000, bar manager Greg Ball sat at the counter one night after closing, chatting with a sous-chef about the ghost. He commented that it would be exciting if the spirit would just do something. As he said that, they heard a loud noise coming from downstairs. Ball went to investigate and had walked partway down the stairs when he saw a chair facing him in the middle of the downstairs area. He swears that the chair had not been there before.

"It was kind of scary. I totally don't dig ghosts," says Ball. "We dumped the rest of our beers and got out of there."

In another instance, a server went to the downstairs bathroom one night to find all the bathroom stall doors swinging open and closed. Then Chef Adrian McCormack arrived early to an empty restaurant and heard footsteps. Rather than get upset, the former Londoner chose to greet the ghost with a cheery "good morning."

Where does the ghost come from? No one really knows, but there's speculation that it might be the spirit of someone who died in a fire that destroyed an Anglican church on the site in 1886. Or, it could be that the spirit is connected to a piece of the wall from the famous St. Valentine's Day massacre, a piece that until 2000 had been in the men's room. Could it be that one of the victims from that horrible event transferred his energy to a new location?

Owner Corinne Lea says the whole thing still feels creepy. "You feel like a kid. You don't want to go down to the basement."

Some of the employees pooh-pooh the ghost theory. Daniel Bacon's birthday is October 30, and he says that, as a Scorpio born just before Halloween, he is not afraid of anything. Still, with a little prodding, he admits that the Scary Room (as the staff call it) freaks him out. It's a room in the back stairwell used to store cleaning supplies and other odds and ends.

"It's a rhomboid shape, skinny at the entrance. There are cobwebs, and it's hard to find the light switch. It's scary, even to me."

Push a little more and Bacon admits that there have been times when he is the last one in the restaurant, and he can't set the alarm system to close up because of "movement" in the downstairs area. The system reads "Not Ready," so Bacon ventures down to check, but no one is ever there. He has had to check the downstairs area three or four times, until the system finally shows "Ready."

"It makes you wonder," says Bacon.

The Falling Phantom
VANCOUVER, BC

The Centre in Vancouver for Performing Arts, formerly known as the Ford Centre, has a remarkable number of ghost stories for such a relatively new building. The 1800-seat theatre on Homer Street, designed by acclaimed Canadian architect Moshe Safdie, opened in 1995 and closed only a few years later because the owners went bankrupt.

While the building sat empty for nearly three years, security teams guarded it 24 hours a day to protect the property from vandals. During those long, lonely shifts, the staff encountered some strange paranormal activity. Elevators would open, close and move between the four floors with no one in them. And two staff members reported repeated incidents in which they heard the sounds of children playing in the basement hallways near the loading bays.

The British Columbia Ghost and Haunting Research Society (BCGHRS) investigated and managed to gather other reports from guards who had worked there. One guard reported seeing some movement on his bank of video monitors while he was working a night shift. He went down to the basement hallways to investigate, thinking perhaps that someone had snuck into the building during the day and had hidden down there. In the basement, he saw a red rubber ball bound across his path, around a corner and out of sight. Seconds later, he heard the footsteps of small children in hot pursuit, and he was bumped by at least two invisible entities as he raced back upstairs to the security office.

More disturbing is the incident recorded on video, which three guards will never be able to erase from their memories. Again, it was a night shift when the strange event happened. One of the guards caught a glimpse on his video monitor of what appeared to be a body plunging past the five-storey glass-walled entrance to the theatre and crashing onto the concrete sidewalk. The guard's response was automatic. He summoned his two colleagues, and they rushed to provide emergency aid to the fallen victim. However, when they arrived outside at the spot where the body should have been, they found nothing out of the ordinary. This alone stunned the guard who had seen the fall because the person should not have been able to crawl away in the short time that it took the guards to arrive on the scene. He certainly would not have been in any shape to walk or run.

Even more unsettling was what they then saw on the video surveillance tapes. The cameras had indeed captured the image of something resembling the horrifying fall that the guard claimed to have seen. According to the guard, as the body was about to hit the ground, it vanished into thin air.

The guards told the BCGHRS researcher that the first falling body incident was definitely not the last. They claimed to have witnessed the startling spectacle at least eight more times over a two-year period, and the building's video cameras recorded each incident. The guards refused to share their videos with the ghost investigators, however, saying that they were being stored for safekeeping.

The revitalized Centre in Vancouver for Performing Arts opened in April 2002, having been purchased by the U.S.-based Four Brothers Entertainment. The current management was contacted to see if the theatre's ghosts continue to "perform" there. An employee named Stacy graciously checked around, but called back to say no one working there now has experienced any paranormal incidents, so it would appear that the ghosts have left or at least have gone into hiding. Many questions remain. Who was the falling person? An unfortunate construction worker? A desperate suicidal jumper? Perhaps it is the work of a spectral stunt master who enjoys the thrill of shocking his human audience time and time again.

Emily's Ghost
at the James Bay Inn
VICTORIA, BC

Emily Carr was a genial, independent and extremely creative Canadian artist and writer. For the staff at the James Bay Inn in Victoria, she remains an awesome and sometimes intimidating presence. Emily's ghost, it seems, has not yet had enough of her hometown.

The historic inn at the corner of Government and Toronto Streets is the third oldest hotel in Victoria, preceded only by the Dominion Hotel and the Empress. Opened in 1911 on a section of Beckley Farm, it has operated continuously as a hotel with only a brief interruption during the war years. The hotel was operated by Mother Cecilia's religious order from 1942 to 1945, as St. Mary's Priory. It was during this period that the hotel welcomed its most famous guest.

Emily Carr had her first heart attack in 1939, and in the years that followed, her health continued to deteriorate until she finally moved from her family home, only a few blocks away, to the guest house for the elderly and infirm. The feisty artist spent her last days at the former hotel, run by the Catholic nuns, the Sisters of the Love of Jesus. While there, Emily Carr had a fatal heart attack at age 73, on March 2, 1945. She is buried in the Carr family plot at the Ross Bay Cemetery.

The area of the inn where Emily lived is now the men's washroom in the bar at the James Bay Inn Pub. She painted in what is now the upstairs lobby and passersby would see her selling her paintings out on the corner sidewalk. Death, however, did not diminish Emily's connection to the inn. Her ghost can be seen from time to time, and staff at the inn often claim to hear her rattling about the building.

Camiel had been on staff for just over a year, working at the front desk and in housekeeping. She said that it's "very creepy" when she is alone, either in the early morning or late at night. "Lots of scary things have happened since I began here."

In December 2002, Camiel was meeting with her boss, Steve, in the small office area behind the front desk. It's a space just big enough for a couple of desks and chairs and a small safe, with a large cutout service window that faces the front door. Steve got up to get something, and Camiel was sitting about five or six feet from the front desk counter when for no reason the silver bell on the counter rang—not once, but twice.

"It was the strangest thing," says Camiel. "I went over to examine the bell, shook it, tapped it from the side, but there was no way to get it to ring without hitting the top of it." She still can't quite fathom it, but it felt as if someone or something must have been trying to get her attention. While I stood at the front desk counter, I tried the bell myself. It's one of those typical metal tapper bells you see on any dry-cleaning shop counter. I shook it, waved my notepad over it and tapped its side. It didn't make a sound until I actually tapped the little button on the top.

Just a month after the bell incident, Camiel had an experience during an early shift that left her shaking. It was around 8:30 AM, and the inn was quiet. She and Jasmine, another employee, were cleaning in the bar.

Camiel recalls, "I was doing housekeeping in the men's washroom. We were trying to get the music to play—there's a digital cable stereo in the bar. We had it on a hip-hop station, and it suddenly switched to Christian rock." Surprised, they went to the stereo and turned it back to the hip-hop station. Within moments, the radio switched again by itself to gentler jazz tunes. "Now we were getting freaked. I mean, the radio can't change unless someone changes it," says Camiel.

The pair reset the radio one more time. In even less time, it just switched off. "We just looked at each other and got the heck out of there." Camiel insists that there is no way to change the station, much less turn the radio off without actually doing it manually. "You have to actually push the buttons. I guess Emily had other ideas about what music should be playing."

Even though a picture of Emily Carr hangs in tribute in the lounge, maybe Emily's spirit is slightly offended that her final home now houses a bar, or perhaps she just enjoys a good joke, adding herself to the list of available spirits.

Eric, a bartender at the inn for 12 years, says he's experienced "plenty of poltergeisty things." One night, something or someone Eric couldn't see was playing games with him. He was walking from behind the bar when he distinctly felt a hand grab his thigh.

"It wasn't a muscle cramp. It was a hand. I could feel it squeezing." The nearest person to him was a waitress about four feet away. He reacted to the squeeze, saying, "Hey, what are you doing?" Then he realized that both her hands were on the bar, and she was out of reach. About a minute later, he was grabbed a second time. "I told the waitress, and we both went, 'Oooo, this is weird.' "

Then there was the inflatable chair incident. A large promotional gimmick, the chair had been lashed to a hook in the ceiling in the corner of the bar. Eric says they tied it securely to ensure it didn't fall on a customer.

That night, a different waitress and Eric were talking about how it had been a while since anything eerie had happened, and she wondered aloud about what Emily's spirit would be up to next.

"Just seconds later, the suspended chair fell right next to her. We were all shocked. It wasn't tied with some hokey knot, so how did that come down?" Eric wonders.

"Now, whenever anything goes wrong we always say, 'Oh, it's just Emily,' " explains Eric.

Another bartender, Laurel, witnessed something that shocked her. A rather inebriated male patron had gone to the bathroom, and upon returning he made a crass comment about urinating on Emily Carr. Laurel put a new drink down on the counter for the man and watched stunned as the glass moved by itself and dumped its contents all over the rude man.

Lynn is a pragmatic woman who has worked both the front desk and night audit for two years. She admits, "You hear things, such as footsteps on the upper floors when no one is around. I've heard the front door open and close. It's an old door; the handle rattles and the door is heavy, so there's no mistaking the sound. But no one goes past."

Down in the bar, Eric echoes Lynn's stories. The doors all have their own distinct squeaks, and many times he has heard the unmistakable sound of the door opening and closing. The door is around a corner, so Eric waits for the person to appear, but often no one is there.

"One night not long ago, it happened twice in five minutes. The waitress heard it too," says Eric. "So after the second time, I rushed over to the door and peered outside, but no one was even near the parking lot. That was freaky."

For Lynn, Emily was simply the unseen reason behind the eerie creaking of an empty hallway floor—that is, until the fall of 2002.

"Then I got scared," says Lynn. "I was going up the stairs to the third floor. I reached the second floor landing and rounded the corner of the stairwell, and as my eyes came level with the third floor, I saw the bottom part of a skirt glide by." She knew by the style that it was an old-fashioned skirt. "But I could see right through it. The hair on the back of my neck and all the hairs on my arms stood up." After that, Lynn was more cautious, taking a powerful flashlight with her on her rounds.

Lynn isn't the only staff member to have seen Emily's ghost. Steve, the office manager, arrived at work early one morning. He parked in the lot next to the building and as he walked from the parking lot to the front door, past the long expanse of hotel windows, he could see a woman in the kitchen. He thought nothing of it, assuming the cook was also in early. Twenty minutes later, the cook came to him asking for the keys to the kitchen.

"So nobody was in the kitchen. That was interesting," says Steve, who admits to not really believing in ghosts. But he concedes, "Any other building, I wouldn't have thought anything of it, but given our history, it's odd."

Emily may not be the only entity enjoying the inn's genteel surroundings. Could it be she has invited a few otherworldly friends to hang out with her? During the summer of 2002, a gentleman guest staying in the two-bedroom cottage that adjoins the inn came to the front desk in an agitated state. He asked Lynn if the inn was haunted. She told him that the ghost of Emily Carr was said to exist in the main building.

The man absorbed that and then asked, "But what about the cottage?"

Everyone in his group had gone out, and he took the opportunity to lie down for a nap.

He told Lynn, "I could hear people moving around talking. I got up and called out but no one was there."

He lay down again, only to be awakened by what sounded like a party. He checked, found nothing and went back to bed. The sounds persisted. He heard laughter, and the floor creaked as if people were walking about. Realizing the party would continue, the disgruntled man finally gave up on his nap.

"I'm generally not superstitious," says Lynn, "but when I go into the bar area at night I call out, 'Hi Emmie, it's just me.' "

Camiel confesses with a laugh that she does the same.

Lynn admits, "That place after hours scares me to death. Even when I put the key in the door, all the hairs on my arms stand up."

Lynn took me on a tour of the bar, which because of the slope of the land is actually the bottom floor of the inn. She's right. At night, the spacious room with its many angles and mirrored walls would be perfect for spooking anyone with an active imagination. When I was there I didn't notice anything peculiar or sense any energy, but perhaps it was Emily's day off.

The Man-Loving Ghost
ABBOTSFORD, BC

In the early 1980s, a woman in Abbotsford discovered that death does not necessarily end a woman's attraction to the opposite sex. Janice Greenwood told the *Vancouver Province* that a ghost lived with her and her roommate, but the female phantom preferred the roommate's boyfriend, to the point of actually crawling into bed with him.

When I contacted Janice, she said what happened is as fresh to her now as it was 20 years ago. Janice explained that four people lived in the house at the time, two upstairs and a couple in the downstairs suite. All four had encounters with the entity.

"We knew the ghost was a woman because we would smell her," says Janice. They would often sniff the distinctive fragrance of strong, flowery perfume, but it was not a scent that any of them wore.

Janice's roommate Cathy had a boyfriend at the time, and he would often stay overnight. Because Cathy worked as a nurse, she often had to get up early for her shift. One morning, Cathy's boyfriend stayed in bed to sleep a little longer. He woke up to the scent of perfume, and he felt someone in the bed next to him. Thinking his girlfriend had slept in, he rolled over to wake her, only to discover no one there. Spooked, the boyfriend got up, put on his clothes and quickly left the house.

"He couldn't get out of there fast enough," says Janice. "The ghost scared the heck out of him."

Smelling the spectre was not the only clue to its presence. Janice and Cathy often found the house unlocked after

192 Canadian Ghost Stories Vol. II

they had locked it, arriving home to find the front door wide open.

"Sometimes when we'd come home, all the lights would be on and the stereo would be blasting. I mean blasting."

Cathy heard someone running up and down the stairs between floors one night and went to see who it was, but the stairwell was empty.

The women had kittens that served as feline phantom sensors. Janice says, "For no reason, the fur would stand up on their backs, and they would start hissing and spitting, although we could see nothing."

One weekend they were dog-sitting for a friend, and the animal spent the entire weekend whimpering and shaking. "We didn't know what to make of it. The dog was freaked out."

Janice had her own experience one day while running herself a bath. As she leaned over the tub to check the water temperature, she felt a strong pressure on her back. "It almost knocked me into the tub," she recalls. "I had to push back, and when I turned around no one was there." At the time she downplayed the incident in her own mind, assuming it was her imagination. But as the list of odd occurrences grew, she came to admit that they lived with a ghost.

Then the man living in the downstairs suite actually saw the ghost. One night, he thought he saw his girlfriend exercising in the living room. Ready for bed after a long day, he told her that it was late and that she should come to bed. He went off to the bedroom, and his girlfriend was already tucked into bed. Stunned, the fellow asked his girlfriend if she had just been exercising in the living room. She said she hadn't been exercising and that she had been in bed for some time. Janice says he swears to this day that he saw a woman doing sit-ups on the living room floor.

They lived in the house for about a year, and the eerie antics continued almost from the time they moved in until the day they left. Janice remembers watching television—in the days before remote controls—and the TV would suddenly turn off by itself. She recalls watching a hockey game, and the set shut itself off.

"What was weird, though, is that when we turned it back on, it was on a different channel. That didn't happen in the days before remotes. If you turned the TV off, it turned back on to the same channel."

Finally, the two roommates decided to try talking to the ghost. "We sat in the living room and started talking out loud. We told the ghost that she was lost, and that she needed to go back, that she didn't belong here," says Janice. "We said, 'You have to leave. You can't keep doing this to us; there's nothing here for you.' " But the ghost stayed.

Janice says they decided that they were sharing their house with a nice ghost "because she never did anything to hurt us." But she admits, "That didn't stop me from putting a large deadbolt on my bedroom door."

After they moved out, they looked into the history of the house to see if some explanation existed for the ghost, but they didn't find anything. Janice also checked with the new people who lived there, and they said they'd had no problems.

"I don't know what to make of it," she admits. "People laughed at us when we said the house was haunted, but we all know what we smelled and heard and saw."

Janice says she heard that spirits don't necessarily have to be connected to the house because of its history to stay there.

"I think our ghost was lost. I had the sense that she was con-fused and didn't know where to go."

Perhaps after the roommates moved out and on to a new phase of their lives, their phantom roomie also chose to move on.

The Thetis Lake Monster
VICTORIA, BC

Picture this. It's a hot August day, perfect for relaxing by a tree-sheltered lake. Suddenly, a horrible gilled creature with shining scales and bulbous eyes rises out of the water, gur-gling ominously. It might be natural to assume some local film company is shooting a remake of *Creature from the Black Lagoon*, until the beast heads towards you and you realize that no cameras are in sight. That was the heart-pounding experi-ence of two teenage boys at Thetis Lake.

For hundreds of years, Indian lore told of encounters with various races of man-eating humanoids that inhabited lakes, rivers and oceans. Some of these monsters are making mod-ern reappearances and scaring the living daylights out of unsuspecting witnesses.

The Thetis Lake Monster resurfaced in the 1970s. The beast, described in detail in Haden Blackman's *The Field Guide to North American Monsters*, is said to be similar in appearance to the gilled, man-like creatures in South America made famous by movies such as *The Swamp Thing*. Tough, silvery scales cover its body and a razor-sharp fin like a crest sticks out from the top of its skull. Added to this delightful ensemble are dark, fish-like bulbous eyes capable of seeing in even the murkiest lake water. The creature has large webbed ears and webbed, clawed hands and feet that allow it to swim at amazing speeds under water.

According to the lore, the monster survives on land and in water because it can somehow extract oxygen from both air and water. It does not have the ability to speak, though its horrible, gurgling noises manage to convey its intent. Those sounds may be a result of forcing water through whatever it uses for lungs.

The first modern sighting of the Thetis Lake Monster occurred on August 19, 1972. Local RCMP officers recorded the account from two terrified teenagers who claimed to have seen the scaly, humanoid form rising from the water while they stood on the lakeshore. The boys ran for their lives, but the monster chased them, getting close enough to cut one boy's hand with the barbed fin of its skull. Police officers taking their testimony were so convinced that the boys' harrowing tale was sincere that they launched an investigation into the attack. Initially, they found no evidence to support the boys' story. However, only four days later, two more witnesses came forward, having been frightened by the same monster. The RCMP redoubled its efforts to track the threatening lake thing, but came up empty-handed. After weeks of searching, in both the lake and the adjacent forest, the police called off their investigation.

There have not been any recent sightings of the Thetis Lake Monster; however, there is also nothing to suggest that the creature departed. As Blackman suggests, anyone thinking of going on a research expedition should be aware that the monster is not likely to greet intruders warmly. Be on the lookout for webbed footprints or discarded scales. And it might be wise to take a flaming torch or some other means of making fire. The body of wisdom surrounding such beasts suggests that these aquatic creatures don't like flames and may be deterred by someone brandishing fire. You just might want to wear your best running shoes as well.

The Townhouse Spectres
VANCOUVER, BC

Strange happenings at a townhouse complex near SE Marine Drive in Vancouver drove the alarmed residents to seek the services of regional ghost investigators. After two visits and detailed research, the British Columbia Ghost and Hauntings Research Society reported not only sufficient evidence of current ghostly activity, but also indications that the root of the situation may be hundreds of years old, tied to the history of the land on which the townhouses are built. Residents in six of the units claim to have had peculiar experiences with the paranormal. These experiences range from detecting mysterious smells and the sound of footsteps to seeing shadowy figures and feeling invisible hands tug at clothes.

The complex near Champlain Heights consists of 70 housing units built in the early 1990s. To protect the privacy of current residents, I will not name the property and will use pseudonyms for the residents (the same names used on the BCGHRS website).

One of the first residents to speak out about the eerie activity was "Donna." She and her family were among the first residents to move into the development and they stayed for eight years, living in two different townhouses. Donna says that she noticed odd incidents almost from the time they arrived.

"But I didn't want to admit it," she says. "Things were constantly disappearing, everything from cutlery to my birth control pills."

A fork or spoon was one thing, but the frequent disappearance of her pills became an issue. The packages would often vanish from their usual spot on a countertop whenever someone left the room. Donna even tried locking them in a drawer but they still disappeared. Finally, thinking another resident might be breaking into her home to play a cruel joke, Donna raised the subject at a meeting of the strata council. After that, other members of the complex admitted they, too, had some strange stories to share.

"Meghan" had heard footsteps walking up the stairs when no one else was in the house. Lights and water faucets turned on and off without anyone present. She also had a picture frame that vibrated persistently. The silver-coloured frame stood about eight inches high and folded on central hinges. Meghan kept the frame on a bedside dresser, and several times a month she would wake up to the sound of it rattling loudly. At first she blamed the heavy traffic passing her home, but she soon realized that only the frame shook. Everything else on the dresser remained still. Meghan tried to shake the dresser to replicate the vibration but couldn't. Unnerved, she threw the picture frame out. Unfortunately, the paranormal high jinks didn't stop.

Other residents also reported lights and water faucets that functioned without human help, televisions that turned on and off and auditory phenomena—whispering or disembodied voices.

"I only freaked out once," says Donna. "I had a baby monitor in my children's room. It was 12:01 AM, and all of a sudden I heard a woman whispering into the monitor." Unlike other events, this felt ominous to Donna. "The ghost was clearly saying something. It wasn't interference. It sounded like she was rushed, but she was whispering. She said words but I couldn't make them out." Frightened by the woman's tormented tone, Donna hid under the covers and told her husband to check on the children. He found them fast asleep.

"Joan" experienced one of the more disturbing personal examples of ghostly activity. Invisible hands often tugged at her clothes, similar to the way a young child does when seeking attention. Joan says the tugging hands happened so often that she was frequently reduced to tears.

When Donna and her family moved to a larger townhouse in the complex while expecting twins, the paranormal activity followed. Twice she heard a glass breaking, but found no broken shards when she went to check. She often smelled the distinctive scents of Old Spice cologne and a strong floral perfume and saw dark shadows in the hallway that made her fearful.

"The shadow would go from the front door, down the hall, past the kids' room, swishing by too quickly for me to put a form to it," Donna recalls. The sightings happened so often that eventually Donna classed them as routine.

But there was obviously nothing routine about the townhouse complex, and in October 2001 the BCGHRS got involved, investigating the history of the land and performing an onsite evaluation. The society's president, Heather

Anderson, says that what they found allowed them to say "there's something strange in the neighbourhood."

The group began its onsite research at Meghan's place, with Donna present. They took audio recordings and photographs in various rooms, as well as around the complex grounds and in the common room used for meetings and social events. Nothing out of the ordinary was recorded; however, one photograph did reveal something extremely unusual.

The photo was taken after a Ouija session that Meghan and Donna held to try to contact whatever spirits might be present. (The BCGHRS notes that it does not support or endorse Ouija activities and did not encourage the session.) During the session, the women communicated with a personality named Jama. The spirit claimed to be a Native male who lived in the area around 1825 and died after falling off a ladder. The investigators prodded Jama—through Meghan and Donna—for answers to some specific questions about the land. Jama revealed that he knew of an accident in 1889 involving a tree that fell, killing four people. The spirit implied that the falling tree had not been an accident, but may have been deliberate. To a request for a picture, Jama said that he could be photographed next to a painting hanging on a nearby wall. The painting showed a picnic for high-society men and women during the 1800s at a lakeside setting.

The resulting photo, according to the group's field notes, was saturated with a semitransparent tan-coloured haze. The ghost team claims this sort of phenomenon has occurred with other supposedly haunted locations. Looking through the haze, they could see a white shape in the middle of the shot. As well, a whitish streak can be seen emanating from the painting and moving past one of the investigator's heads, pooling in a series of miniature vortexes just above the Ouija board. The strange streaks were also on the negatives, and as the field notes record, "do exist in three-dimensional space— the curvature from the painting clearly goes around John's head, not through it or over top of it."

What struck the ghost research team was the connection between Jama's statements and historical fact. Their research uncovered that hundreds of years ago, the ancestral relatives of today's Squamish, Burrard and Musqueam First Nations bands used the Killarney region for their summer residence. The area was favoured for its lush forests, abundant wildlife and proximity to the Fraser River. It also became popular with British settlers in the 1800s, and though it is not recorded, there may have been violent conflicts between the bands and white settlers. With the onset of logging, the Native people were likely forced off the land by the govern-ment to make way for industry.

In 1868, British surveyor William Henry Rowling was granted a large portion of the region. His land extended along the riverfront to just past where the townhouse com-plex is situated. Rowling, his wife, Mary, and their five young children became the first settlers in South Vancouver, accord-ing to city records.

During Christmas celebrations in 1889, Rowling hosted a party at one of the three houses he had built on the property. The festivities came to a tragic conclusion when a horse-drawn buggy containing several young guests met a terrible fate. Archival documents show that as the buggy travelled along North Arm Road that ran through Rowling's land, a massive tree fell on it. James Bodwell, Clarence Campbell,

James Lawson and Jasper Locke were crushed to death. Lawson's younger sister Mayo received minor injuries and miraculously survived, along with another passenger who was unharmed. The *Daily Colonist* article on December 27, 1889, recounted the accident: "The news of the sad affair cast a gloom over this city and the North Arm, all the parties being well known. The bodies were crushed and mutilated almost beyond recognition."

Heather Anderson says that the women at the Ouija session did not know any of this history, so the investigators were surprised to hear the details emerge from their "conversation" with Jama. Even more shocking was the detail that the tree's fall was deliberate. The research revealed that James Saint, a neighbour and relative newcomer to the area, was believed to be partially responsible for the deaths. A few days earlier, Saint had cut into the tree and filled the massive trunk with hot coals in order to bring it down, a method that was common practice in those days.

Given the sudden, tragic deaths and the previous uprooting of Native people from land that may have included burial sites, not to mention subsequent urban development including a landfill in the 1950s, it seems the townhouse development is a sure bet for a haunting.

The story doesn't end there. One of the BCGHRS investigators returned to the complex in November 2001 and encountered disembodied footsteps and the sound of someone pacing in Meghan's home. No one else was staying at the home, and both Meghan and the researcher heard the sound of someone running up the stairs just as they entered the house. The sounds seemed consistent with the noise a small child would make running, not a heavy pounding, but just enough body weight to make the steps squeak. And recently, one of the other residents came forward to say her son has been seeing the spirits of children.

The woman told Donna, "My son has been seeing children, black and white-skinned, and one had a broken arm. They're crying and obviously in distress." The little boy claims to see the small ghosts behind the complex near a wooded area where the kids build tree forts.

Donna says, "It is creepy back there. We used to take our dog for walks but even he would get scared."

The woman was worried because her son started seeing the ghosts in January 2003 and now has trouble going upstairs to bed by himself because he is suddenly afraid of the dark.

Heather Anderson isn't sure how the child wraiths fit into what is going on at the townhouse complex, but she would like to look into it further. They have posted all the information gathered so far on the BCGHRS website.

Says Anderson, "I don't feel this is done by any stretch of the imagination."

6
Québec

King George Park
WESTMOUNT, QC

This intriguing story about King George Park, also known as Murray Park, in the Montréal district of Westmount, was submitted to the Québec Ghosts and Hauntings Research Society. It is with their permission that we include it in this book. The QGHRS would be interested in hearing from anyone else who has had unusual experiences in the park.

This story happened on a frosty fall evening in the late 1970s. Two men driving by the park in the wee hours of the morning stopped to have a cigarette. The night air had cooled to the point where they could see their breath. What they didn't expect to see was a procession of children walking up the hill towards them, chanting something they couldn't make out. The youngsters were not wearing modern clothes but appeared to be traipsing about in nightclothes from a much earlier time period. Some of the older children appeared to have assumed the role of guardian, either carrying the younger ones or holding their hands. No adults accompanied them.

The two friends were stunned that someone would let children out so very late without adult supervision. Then they took note of the unusual clothes. What finally sank in was even more startling. On this chilly October night, the two friends realized that they couldn't see any breath coming from these chanting children. The procession of ghostly girls and boys then walked right by them without acknowledging the open-mouthed pair. The men looked at each other and hurried back to their car. They drove in the same direction that the children had been walking but couldn't see them anywhere. The singing spectres had vanished.

There is nothing obvious about the area's history to explain the children's appearance. The person who supplied the story had checked into records to see if the park site had once been an orphanage or boarding school but found nothing. Perhaps the story is simply an urban myth.

But maybe, as some paranormal experts believe, this was an example of a psychic impression from the past. Unlike a ghost, which is generally believed to be the spirit of a human being who has passed out of his or her physical body but has not passed on to the next realm, a psychic impression is like a well-worn spot on the fabric of time. Ghosts manifest themselves in different ways, but an imprint always appears the same.

Or could it be that the two friends happened upon a rift between this time and an earlier one in which the children continue to play together, still very much alive in their own time dimension?

Maud of the Willow Place Inn
HUDSON, QC

To escape the relentless urban clamour, the citizens of Montréal retreat to the peaceful bliss of Lac des Deux Montagnes, just 45 minutes from the heart of the city. Many stay in the charming country village of Hudson on the south shore of the lake. If they stay at the Willow Place Inn, the seekers of quiet may find their solitude disrupted by a rebellious poltergeist. The ghost of a servant girl murdered by rebels is said to haunt the historic hotel.

The Willow Place Inn holds a significant place in Québec's history. Built in 1820, the attractive two-storey Georgian structure started out as a private residence. It served as a meeting place during the 1837 Rebellion, and it was there that the *Patriote* rebels devised their plan for the uprising at Saint-Eustache, which took place on December 14, 1837. While the *Patriotes* worked out details of their attack, Maud the servant girl took mental notes. As it turns out, Maud's allegiances were with the militia. When the *Patriotes* learned she was a traitor, they murdered Maud to keep her silent and buried her body in the dirt floor of the home's basement. But it seems that a little dirt and a few hundred years could not stop Maud. Her ghost continues to try to get people's attention. Could it be that she still feels compelled to reveal the rebels' plans?

Former employees and visitors claim to have had strange encounters while at the inn. Chairs crash to the floor, knocked over by an unseen hand. The basement door is heard slamming shut by itself. Ex-employees told a television documentary crew in 2002 that going down to the basement is scary. Mushrooms grown down in the cellar area, above the spot where Maud is thought to be buried, are found "beheaded." Employees have also reported finding piles of rocks outside the door of room 8, of hearing someone singing pretty songs when there is no one near or smelling perfume waft by even though no one else is present.

Long-time residents of Hudson are divided over whether there is truly a ghost at the inn. Hudson's historians admit to knowing of local skirmishes between rebels and loyal citizens

The Willow Place Inn is said to be haunted by Maud, a servant girl who was murdered by political rebels.

in 1837, during the time that the area was being settled, so there may be some basis for the story of Maud's murder. However, concrete evidence of her death is scarce, and many scoff at the notion that something supernatural exists at Willow Place Inn. And since the original building burned to the ground in 1989, many people conclude that the ghost is now simply the rural equivalent of an urban legend.

Yet some employees say that even in the new building, which was rebuilt in the style of the former residence, there definitely is a strange atmosphere at times. The disturbances seem to begin at the onset of winter, starting on Halloween night and continuing for one full month. Then, inexplicably, the poltergeist activity stops for another year.

Owner Michael Dobbie is one of those on the fence about Maud's existence. "All I go on is what I've picked up on in the 20 years since I've owned the inn," he says. "I'll be frank with you. There have been so many stories and a lot of intermingling between fact and fiction. Over the years I've heard so much that I have a hard time deciphering the truth myself."

Dobbie hasn't experienced anything personally but says that he has had several guests who came down "in a frenzy" after witnessing something strange.

"There have been a number of those things over the years," Dobbie says. Cold spots in some rooms have startled the guests. They felt a cold draft move by like someone passing them on a still, warm night. Other guests complained of hearing noises in the hall, and when they went to check, no one was there. They would be doubly distressed upon discovering that they were alone in the inn that night. Dobbie has also heard of furniture being moved, but rumours of the decapitated mushrooms caught him by surprise.

"That's a new one on me." He can't recall exactly when the last paranormal event occurred, although he knows one occurred after the fire. "I take it for granted now," he says. "I've stopped keeping track."

One front desk receptionist has worked at the inn for 13 years and says that, despite all the stories, she hasn't seen Maud. "I grew up in Hudson, and I remember the old inn and hearing stories about Maud, but I can't say I've been affected by her."

She surmises that Maud moved on after the old structure was destroyed. Perhaps after the whole story was televised in a Canadian program dedicated to ghost stories, *Creepy Canada*, Maud felt her truth had finally been told and she was free to continue on to the next plane.

Montréal's Ghosts
MONTRÉAL, QC

At least half a dozen ghosts roam the streets and buildings of Montréal. Many are the stuff of legends, tied to the city's history. Others are a result of trauma or accident that ties them to this plane. But if you hear the distinct sound of wooden wheels on cobblestones or the smart click of soldiers' boots marching, you may have run into some of Montréal's paranormal parade.

To give the ghosts a historical context, the fledgling community, founded by Jacques Cartier in 1535, grew as a part of New France until it was taken over by British troops in 1760. In 1792, the town was divided into two sections, east and west, along the length of Saint Laurent Street. The first streetlights appeared on Saint Paul Street in 1815, and McGill University received its charter in 1821. In 1833, after the city was incorporated, Jacques Viger was elected Montréal's first mayor. Montréal's prominence as a port led to its rapid development as an industrial city, and by the time of confederation in 1867, the city was the capital of commerce and trade in the new country.

One of the better-known legends concerns a phantom calèche that still offers service to unwitting travellers on Saint Paul Street during the early morning hours. The carriage pulls up, and the driver solicits passengers, offering to take them home. But the carriage vanishes into thin air when anyone tries to step into it.

Just across Lachine Rapids, the ghosts of military men haunt an area around the Old Fort on Île Ste-Hélène. Samuel

Given its rich history, it's no surprise that Montréal has an abundance of ghosts.

de Champlain named the island in honour of his wife, Hélène de Champlain, née Boullé. The Le Moyne family of Longueuil owned the island from 1665 to 1818, when they sold it to the British government. The government built the fort, powder house and blockhouse on the island after the War of 1812. In 1870 the Canadian government acquired it and transformed it into a public park in 1874. Currently, a museum holds a re-creation of military times past, with the Compagnie Franche de la Marine showcasing the period from 1683 to 1760, while the Fraser Highlanders re-create the 78th Regiment that served in Canada from 1757 to 1763. However, the sound of troops marching at midnight is not part of the show. Several witnesses claim to have heard marching sounds, "as though people were marching to a meeting." The sounds always start at midnight and finish at sunrise. As well, the ghost of a French soldier has been reported visiting an antique shop. I spoke to current members of the Fraser Highlanders, and they found the tales interesting, but no one had seen or heard anything out of the ordinary.

But Montréal's legends don't end there. In 1763, Marie-Josephe Corriveau was hanged as a witch for the murder of her husband. After the execution, her body was placed in an iron cage and hung out on public display until it decomposed. The cage is now part of the collection at the Château de Ramezay, a handsome stone mansion built by Montréal's 11th governor, Claude de Ramezay, and now used as a museum. According to the legend, "La Corriveau" is doomed to return to that cage for one night each year. The night, rather predictably, is October 31. Staff members at the museum say that they haven't noticed anything strange recently involving the cage, and given that it is now in storage, it is unlikely that anyone would see the ghost even if she did return.

At McGill University, people tell stories of ghosts on the downtown campus. In the medical faculty, a few people say they have observed a man with a long black coat and top hat wandering the second floor of the building. And the spirit of furrier Simon McTavish is said to haunt the upper regions of the McGill campus at McTavish Street and Pine Avenue. Unfortunately, there is no information available as to how

The haunting at the Château de Ramezay is connected to Marie-Josephe Corriveau, who was executed for killing her husband.

McTavish's ghost appears or if there have been recent sightings. So for this book, the story may fall into the category of urban myth.

John Abbott College, named after Canada's third prime minister, is in Sainte-Anne-de-Bellevue, on the western tip of the island of Montréal. The college has six renovated early 20th-century buildings that sit at the edge of Lac Saint-Louis.

The college is considered to have one of the most beautiful campuses in Québec, and it also bears the distinction of being haunted. Security guards at the college have reported finding doors swinging open that were locked when checked just moments earlier. Lights are often found on after being turned off. One of the current security guards says he has heard the stories and rumours of the John Abbott spirit. "Weird things are supposed to occur, that kind of thing. No one is sure who the ghost is, or even if it is male or female." He adds, "None of our officers have ever encountered anything. We've just heard the rumours."

On Bleury, between Ste-Catherine and De Maisonneuve, Montréal's historic Imperial Theatre has kept up with the times with its cinematic fare, but it seems to have a ghost that dates back to its original vaudeville days. The Imperial opened to the public on April 26, 1913. The vaudeville house was fitted with its own Wurlitzer organ and could pack 2000 people in to see live performances of dancers, cabaret acts and comedians. The Imperial also got on the moving pictures bandwagon, and in 1928 became one of the first theatres in the city to present films with sound. In the late 1920s, a fire started in the projection booth on the second-floor balcony, and apparently a ballerina died in the blaze. Recently, many employees have reported hearing footsteps when they are alone in the theatre. Also, doors that are carefully locked at night are found mysteriously unlocked the next morning.

Could the unfortunate dancer still be practising her pirouettes and unlocking the door to make sure others can get out if they have to?

There are a few ways to track down Montréal's spooky secrets. Tours of Old Montréal will uncover the legends,

The spirit of a ballerina at the historic Imperial Theatre dates back to the days of vaudeville.

unexplained phenomena and ghosts that haunt the cobbled streets. And the very brave may wish to take a stroll after sundown. Who knows what famous figure or former war hero might cross your path?

The Centaur Theatre
MONTRÉAL, QC

Situated among the cobblestone streets of Old Montréal, the historic Centaur Theatre is a jewel in the city's theatre crown. A haunted jewel, that is. It seems that the soul of some former financier may still be chained to a desk in the afterlife.

Who says money and the arts don't mix? Montréal's leading English-language theatre company makes its home in Canada's first stock exchange building. The stunning example of Beaux Arts architecture on Saint François-Xavier Street was designed by American architect George B. Post (creator of the New York Stock Exchange building) and completed in 1904. The glorious edifice contained the Montréal Stock Exchange until 1965. Four years later, the Centaur Theatre turned the former financial bastion into a first-class performance space. The building now houses two theatres, the Seagram's art gallery and lounge, administrative and production facilities and a fully computerized box office system. Shortly after the theatre company set up shop, reports began surfacing that the building was haunted.

Unlike most theatre ghosts, this particular spirit is tied to the building's previous function. Apparently, the spirit manifests itself by shuffling papers as if in an eternal time crunch. People have also reported hearing music when there is none being played.

In 1991, the Centaur's publicist told the *Montréal Gazette*, "Rumour has it that the ghost has something to do with the vaults that were used when the building was the stock exchange." The vaults are still down there, and perhaps the ghost is some harried stockbroker from those days.

One person who might offer a clue is Front of House Manager Layne Shutt. He says that during his 12 years at the theatre he certainly has heard theories that the ghost may be the spirit of a harried stockbroker who committed suicide, but he's inclined to think that the spirit may actually be that of a child. He explained that in the early days of the stock exchange, the only telegraph in the area was in the CPR building across the street. Apparently, the traders hired small children as "runners" to gather the ticker tape information as it came across the wire and then hustle it across to the exchange. Small balconies ringed the trading floor, and the children delivered the quotes to the men on the balconies, who wrote the information on chalkboard-covered walls.

"The story I heard," says Shutt, "is that one of the kids tripped while on the balcony and fell to the trading floor, breaking his neck." He says of the strange events that defy explanation, "The things that happen here are not evil or dark. They're more like the pranks of a trickster, the things a kid would do, not a 50-year-old stockbroker."

Shutt has some experience with ghosts. During a stint at Montréal's Black Theatre Workshop, he recalls that every week for about six months, he and others working there heard the front door open and slam shut, followed by the sound of someone walking up the stairs and down the hall to the office.

"But no one was ever there."

In addition, one night at a dinner party in his home, he told the story to his guests. At the end of the story, the clock on his bookshelf bonged twice, making everyone jump and laugh at the perfect timing of it striking the hour just as the story concluded.

"The only problem was the clock didn't have a chime, and it wasn't wound," says Shutt.

Shutt's personal experience with the Centaur Theatre's spectre is a doozy. "This is the story I tend to tell when people ask me about the ghost. I think people expect this place to be haunted."

It happened about five years ago, late one evening when Shutt was making his rounds. Part of his job is to walk through the entire building every night and ensure all the doors are locked. In the basement there is a long hallway running from the north to the south end of the building, with doors that lead off to various rooms. At the extreme north end are the sound room and costume shop, the green room and then a series of dressing-room doorways for one of the two theatre spaces. At the other end of the hall, there is the prop shop, storage and maintenance. At the extreme south end is the workshop. "I usually start at one end and work my way down the hall," says Shutt. "The actors rarely close their doors, and for fire regulations we have to make sure all doors are shut."

On this particular night, Shutt recalls that it was unusually late, around 3:30 AM. "I started at the north end and locked all the doors. I finally got to the south end and locked the workshop door." Tired and ready to go home, he was stunned by what greeted him when he turned around. "Every single door was wide open." Shutt had not heard a single lock turn, and he knows he was the only person in the building, let alone in the basement hallway. "I cursed and then I admit I got a little spooked. When you lock these doors with a key, you need a key to unlock them. It's the fire regulations that you can't have a self-locking door." He locked them all again and hurried home.

Other phantom pranks Layne Shutt says he has heard about but can't corroborate. A set designer complained that, while trying to paint the stage, someone or something kept tipping over his buckets of paint. The designer had filled one bucket, and turned to work on something else. When he looked back, the bucket was lying on its side with the paint spilled. He cleaned the mess and refilled the bucket, only to have it spill again.

"Nine times out of ten I'm the last one in the building," says Shutt. "There's a lot of corner-of-your-eye stuff. You see something whiz by, so you stop to look, and there's nothing there. I've heard that quite a bit from other staff as well."

This year the Centaur Theatre celebrates the building's 100th anniversary. Perhaps the ghost may take it as an opportunity to bid farewell to the 21st century and move on to another plane. Or maybe the child spirit enjoys playing its eternal games and will hang around for another century.

The Ghost of Mary Gallagher
MONTRÉAL, QC

One of Montréal's better-known legends is that of prostitute Mary Gallagher. The streetwise strumpet plied her trade in the area known as Griffintown—the Irish working-class district of the city. She was murdered on June 26, 1879, when a jealous colleague cut her head off. Every seven years since Mary Gallagher's murder, residents of the "Griff," as locals call it, arrive at the scene of the crime on the corner of Murray and William Streets to watch for her ghost. It is said to walk the streets of the Irish heart of Montréal in search of her missing noggin.

It was a warm June night in 1879, and the streets of Griffintown teemed with the sights and sounds of the burgeoning industrial age. The daytime noises and acrid smoke emanating from the steel foundries, the cotton and sugar mills, the Grand Trunk Railway yards and the Lachine canal had faded away. The streets resonated with the sounds of Irish shopkeepers and tavern owners hawking their wares in their gas-lit shops.

On William Street in the heart of Griffintown, many a worker tried to drown the memory of his 14-hour day in cheap whisky. Near midnight, three drunken souls staggered up the steps to a second-floor flat. Twenty-three-year-old Susan Kennedy, who by all accounts was well versed in the ways of the "oldest profession," occupied the William Street residence. Accompanying Kennedy were her friend, colleague and soon-to-be rival, 38-year-old Mary Gallagher, and their latest trick, a young factory worker named Michael Flanagan.

In the poor, working-class neighbourhood of Griffintown, prostitute Mary Gallagher was brutally slain.

The three had met at a small hotel near the Bonsecours Market, where Susan and Mary had gone earlier that afternoon in search of a little excitement. The women had polished off two bottles of whisky together before striking up a conversation with the dashing Mr. Flanagan. Eventually the trio made the fateful journey to Susan's house.

As the night wore on, the two women increasingly vied for the attentions of the handsome Irishman, until it became clear to Kennedy that Flanagan was more interested in her much older friend and a bottle of whisky than in her own amorous advances. After drinking with Gallagher for about an hour, Flanagan passed out on the floor of the flat, sending Kennedy into an intoxicated jealous rage. After knocking Mary Gallagher out, she took a hand axe from the kitchen and proceeded to chop off Mary's head in a series of blunt awkward strokes. After some 10 minutes of hacking, Kennedy disposed of the grisly trophy in a water pail beside the kitchen sink.

Police charged Susan Kennedy and Michael Flanagan with the gruesome homicide, but during the trial it became clear that only one pair of hands had wielded the murder weapon. Kennedy's blood-soaked clothes and the hatchet were found in her home, and her two alibis contradicted one another. The downstairs neighbour testified that around 12:15 AM she'd heard the sound of a body hitting the floor and then 10 minutes of loud chopping. But it was the damning testimony of Constable William Craig that wrapped up the prosecution's case. Craig told the court that he had arrested Kennedy many times and that sometimes "she was so violent with drink that it took two men to hold her, and she had to be put into a wood cart to be taken to the station."

The jury acquitted Michael Flanagan but found Susan Kennedy guilty of the murder. She was sentenced to hang on December 5, 1879. However, Prime Minister John A. Macdonald commuted the sentence in light of evidence presented at the trial, and Kennedy spent 16 years in prison instead. She died in 1916.

Clearly, Mary Gallagher found no peace through justice, since she appears doomed to return eternally to the site of her death. As years passed, the legend grew of her headless form returning every seven years to wander about the district in search of her head. Few documented sightings of her ghost exist, the last one in 1928. Soon after, the Griffintown neighbourhood was demolished to accommodate the O'Keefe breweries. Today, the haunted area is a vacant lot on the southeast corner of William and Murray Streets. People still gather on the anniversary of her murder to see if they will catch sight of the headless spectre.

Some dispute the date of the most recent sighting. At the last Mary Gallagher evening in June 1998, one regular watcher says that not only did she see Mary's ghost, but she also received a message from her! Up until this strange event, the evening had run true to form—Mary was a no-show, and the group gave up the ghost, so to speak, by 10 PM and headed to the nearby pubs in search of more satisfying spirits. The woman remained behind, and after everyone had gone she looked up to where the second-floor flat used to be.

Feeling very foolish, she whispered, "Mary Gallagher, are you there?" A cloud covered the moon, and emboldened by the darkness, she asked again more loudly.

Suddenly, a shimmering building of red bricks appeared on the empty lot. On the Murray Street side, a second-floor window shone with lamplight, and a shadowy figure called out, "Get away from here now! Don't you know I'm no longer in the scarlet trade? Besides, you look as if you haven't a shilling to your name."

As if that wasn't shocking enough, the shadowy figure continued her rant. "My body would be of no use to you now, for it's dust. The only way I could rise again would be as a flower if they used my dust as fertilizer."

The next scheduled appearance of Mary Gallagher is June 26, 2005. Whether she'll show up is anyone's guess. It's like the theory behind buying lottery tickets—if you aren't there, you won't know.

The Ghost of the Cathedral
QUÉBEC CITY, QC

For followers of supernatural phenomena, Québec has more religious manifestations than any other region in the country. Perhaps it is because of the strong influence of the Church on the province's history, but whatever the reason, Québec has recorded some incredible poltergeist shenanigans. Topping the list for one local ghost tour operator is Québec City's Holy Trinity Cathedral, where icy chills and phantom figures have frightened several church organists and a few tour guides.

The historic church on Rue des Jardins in Québec City was the first Anglican cathedral to be built outside of the British Isles. King George III paid for its construction, which began on August 11, 1800, and was completed four years later. Unlike the colourful splendour of baroque churches, the cathedral was modelled on London's famous St. Martin's-in-the-Fields for a look described as well-bred classical austerity. The architects hoped that the plain design would be soothing to parishioners. But having a ghost seems to somehow detract from that goal.

Stories of paranormal experiences were first recounted by organists who were in the church alone at night, practising their repertoire. Doors slammed shut, footsteps echoed

Organists and tour guides have reported unsettling paranormal activity at Holy Trinity Cathedral in Québec City.

throughout the cathedral and the shadowy figure of a woman could be seen moving among the pillars. The activity seemed to be at its worst during the month of November. Laurie Thatcher first heard of the tales from one of her guides, who is the daughter of the archbishop. Intrigued, she investigated further and found the spine-tingling stories to be true and terrifying.

One organist told her that he experienced the strange events in a particular order. "It seemed to start with doors banging," he explained. "I knew I was alone but would still get up, walk around and call out to see if someone had snuck into the church. I always locked the entry doors as a precaution, but the interior doors opening and slamming shut were startling." In winter, he would check for footsteps in the snow, but he could never see any sign of someone entering or leaving the building.

Despite the church's central heating, the organist would feel a distinctly icy chill wrap itself around him as he played. He also heard footsteps walking towards him from behind, but invariably when he turned to look, no one was there. All this set the organist's nerves on edge, but the sight of a ghost completely frazzled him. The frightened man told Thatcher that while playing, he looked up to the second-floor balcony. Huge support pillars rise from the floor to the church's ornate ceiling and are spaced about 10 feet apart. "I saw what appeared to be the shadowy form of a woman moving between the pillars," reported the organist.

The strange happenings affected others as well. Another organist took his dog to his practice sessions. At other churches, it had never been a problem because the dog simply curled up and went to sleep. At Holy Trinity, however, the animal ran up and down the aisles snapping at the air.

"My dog had never bitten or showed aggression to anyone in his life," said the man.

A different organist finally gave in to fear and frustration and yelled out to the empty church, "I know you're here!" At his words, the sheet music on the organ lifted up and dropped to the floor, despite a wind guard to prevent the loose sheets from moving.

All these incidents led church officials to an unusual source for assistance. A medium paid the church several visits, and he concluded that the ghostly activity resulted from a tragic murder that took place about 75 years after the cathedral was consecrated. The medium said he felt that a woman from a nearby religious order had become pregnant. After delivering the baby, she killed it to avoid persecution or rejection from the order and then buried the body under the floorboards near the organ. Beneath the organ, there is a crypt that contains the grave of one of the church's first bishops. Next to it is a smaller, unmarked grave. No church records exist to explain who is buried within, but the size indicates it is the grave of a small child. Could it be the tomb of the murdered baby? The medium believes the woman's spirit returns to the church out of guilt and remorse.

Laurie Thatcher included the cathedral on her ghost tour in October 2002, and as her company moves into its second year, she says it is still the wildest and scariest place on the eight-stop tour. Within the first week of going there, Thatcher herself experienced strange things that she has trouble explaining.

"It was as if she knew I was the boss and went right for me," says Thatcher.

The tours take place at night, and one of the features is a candlelit lantern carried by the guide. Thatcher says she set her lantern on a marble table just inside the cathedral door. She locked the entry door and moved through the foyer to unlock the interior doors. When she returned for her lantern, the tea light candle inside was out. She went to re-light it, only to discover the entire candle was missing. "Not just the wax, but the entire foil holder as well. It had disappeared without a trace." To avoid alarming her group, Thatcher told them her matches were wet and finished the tour with an unlit lantern.

The next night, icy fingers crawled up her legs while she tried to tell a tour group the cathedral's story. At first, Laurie Thatcher assumed her imagination was working overtime. After all, she wore a floor-length cloak and should have been comfortably warm. But, she says, when one of the tour members spoke up and asked if anyone else had felt a chill move up their legs, "I almost dropped my lantern."

The strength of the spirit activity seems to allow it to affect areas even beyond the church's walls. While training a guide at the cathedral one afternoon, Thatcher says the novice insisted on seeing the cellar gravesite of the child. After half an hour of exploring the church, the two made the seven-minute walk back to the tour office. Thatcher found her receptionist in a panic. The woman said that about seven minutes after they left for the church (about the time they entered Holy Trinity), all the phone lines went dead. Thatcher checked, and sure enough, no dial tone. She crossed the street, where the phones seemed to be functioning, and called the telephone company. They told her nothing was wrong with the lines. Just then, her receptionist came to say that the phones were back up.

"It was strange. None of my neighbours had any phone problems."

Neither Laurie nor any of her guides has seen the ghost, but she and others have witnessed a fluttery shadow and have had doors slam shut while they were giving the tour speech. The activity shows no signs of slowing down. When the 2003 season opened in May, Thatcher says that one of the guides sensed that the ghost is angry that they are back. For the first time, the guide reported feeling frightened while inside the cathedral.

So all you ghost hunters on the prowl for new paranormal experiences, take note. It might be worth keeping that warning in mind if you are thinking of going to the cathedral for more than just prayer and meditation.

The Hudson Poltergeist
HUDSON, QC

For a tiny village, Hudson commands a lot of ink when it comes to tales of paranormal phenomena. News of an active poltergeist at the Hudson Hotel drew crowds of ghost hunters and curiosity seekers to the community on the banks of the Ottawa River. Mind you, in 1880 such current affairs carried more weight than they might in today's desensitized, sophisticated populace. Even so, the disturbances remain unexplained to this day, and the mystery of the Hudson poltergeist lives on. This tale is included in John Robert Colombo's *Ghost Stories of Canada*.

What set the strange activities at John Park's hotel apart from the regular run-of-the-mill poltergeist pranks was the time at which they occurred. The manifestations took place during the day, rather than under cover of night. Bed linens, mattresses and furniture were found in a shambles, as if someone had flailed through the room during a massive tantrum. The incidents began in the middle of September, and by October 1, 1880, whatever was causing the chaos seemed to be escalating its efforts.

Staff found several empty rooms turned upside down. Beds were overturned, furniture and linens were scattered and locked windows were open. In the kitchen, the cook put down a loaf of bread to go in search of something, only to discover upon returning that the bread had disappeared. After a lengthy search, she found the missing loaf in a laundry basket.

Most of the strange occurrences were annoying but harmless. However, when fire broke out in the stable hayloft, the *curé* of the local parish got a hasty summons. The blaze had nearly consumed the stable and threatened the entire hotel. It was time to take the matter seriously. The priest uttered some prayers and sprinkled holy water about, which seemed to calm the unruly spirit. Unfortunately, the effects lasted only as long as the priest's visit. The minute he left, the poltergeist got right back into its game of disruption.

More mayhem ensued, with more rooms turned upside down and bottles of liquor in the bar moving by themselves. John Park reached his limit of tolerance. He called for another priest on Sunday, October 3, and with a gathered crowd of more than 100 witnesses, the cleric performed an exorcism to remove the spirit.

Finally, life calmed down at the Hudson Hotel. Everything returned to normal, and the spirit never surfaced again. To this day, the mystery of what caused the unusual activity remains unsolved.

The Old Ramsay Chapel
MAGOG, QC

Québec's Eastern Townships have many interesting stories of unusual phenomena. In the city of Magog, on the eastern shore of Lake Memphrémagog, is a picturesque bed-and-breakfast with a decidedly spiritual bent. La Vieille Chapelle Ramsay—the Old Ramsay Chapel—overlooks Magog from its place on the promontory on the south side of the Chemin des Pères. Locals here are used to strange tales. Their lake is home to the famous monster Memphré (which you can read about elsewhere in this book), so it didn't raise too many eyebrows when the owners of the bed-and-breakfast said their work to restore the old chapel was inspired by spirits of the past.

In November 1994, Regina Makuch and Jean-Louis Le Cavalier bought the two-storey mansion, knowing nothing of its history but thinking it would convert into a perfect bed-and-breakfast establishment. Once in the house, Regina began to sense another presence. She also felt it had a different agenda. Regina heard voices and sounds of someone sobbing, prompting her to investigate who might be trying to contact her.

She discovered that the 17-room mansion had belonged to Monsignor David Shaw Ramsay. The Scottish Presbyterian cleric built the home sometime between 1860 and 1880. After settling in Québec, Ramsay converted to Catholicism and was received by the Jesuit order in England in 1867. He returned to Québec to work as chaplain at the Montréal prison, and in 1897 Ramsay took up full-time residence at his Magog mansion, becoming the local parish priest. While having the mansion built, Ramsay ensured it contained the high-ceilinged chapel for conducting both private and public services. He devoutly served his community, and when he died, it seemed that his spirit refused to sever his connection with his flock.

Regina Makuch felt that the Monsignor was communicating with her to try to revive the chapel as a place where his former parishioners could go to pray and meditate. Regina saw visions of the priest and heard his voice instruct her that the restoration work needed to happen quickly. She also sensed that once the guesthouse opened, the efforts to restore the chapel would be rewarded.

In January 1995, the Old Ramsay Chapel opened for business, with three guest rooms and a beautifully refurbished chapel. Makuch and Le Cavalier did a bustling business in the first year, suggesting that the Monsignor still watched over his flock. However, it seems the chapel is now closed. Attempts to reach someone there have been met with messages that the phone number is no longer in service.

The Memphrémagog Monster
NEAR MAGOG, QC

They saw a monster dark and grim
Coming with coiling surge and swim,
With lifted head and tusk and horn,
Fierce as the spirit of Hades born.
—Norman Bingham, *The Sea Serpent Legend,* 1926

Inland sea serpents add a certain flair to any lakeside holiday, and Canada lays claim to several insolent and unexplained underwater monsters. Naturally, central British Columbia's Ogopogo tops the list, and my colleague Barbara Smith provides wonderful detail on its history in *Ghost Stories and Mysterious Creatures of British Columbia*. However, two neighbouring creatures reported to be in Québec have intrigued scientists and skeptics for nearly two centuries.

Lake Memphrémagog extends like a long, thin finger from Magog, Québec, near Sherbrooke, across the border to Newport, Vermont. The deep, cold lake lies in a valley between mountains, and at the base of Owl's Head Mountain resides one of the most famous mysterious creatures in the region. Dubbed Memphré, the sea serpent has been the stuff of local legend since the beginning of the 19th century. And the sightings have not diminished over time. Until the year 2000, 229 experiences were well documented (not including hearsay references). According to research done by Sonia Bolduc of the University of Sherbrooke, approximately eight sightings occur per year, documented by dozens of witnesses.

Stories of a giant sea creature emerged in the latter part of the 18th century. Indians warned the first white settlers not to swim in the lake because of a marine monster. Description of the beast, its level of aggression and where it lives varies, but the common denominator is that something very large and predatory lurks in Memphrémagog's depths. Norman Bingham's poem, quoted above, revives an old Indian legend of two unfortunate lovers who meet a tragic and horrible fate in Memphré's alarming jaws.

In 1816, local settler Ralph Merry documented four sightings by people he deemed credible. Although Merry himself

A mysterious creature called Memphré is said to dwell in the waters of Lake Memphrémagog.

had not seen anything unusual, he carefully noted the details of what witnesses claimed they saw. Their accounts, and the hundreds that followed, generally agreed on the sea serpent's description—it is dark grey or black and measures between 20 and 50 feet long, with a horse-like head and powerful and swift swimming ability.

In 1847, the *Stanstead Journal* reported several occasions of lakeshore sightings by area residents. Over the years, the sea monster surfaced often enough that locals and tourists alike were a little on edge when swimming in or boating alone on the lake.

Then in 1961, two fishermen heading for Newport came to shore shaken by what they swore was a close call. The men said they watched a black creature about 20 feet long swim alongside their boat for more than half a minute. According to their report, the animal had a round back and an oddly shaped head that defied definition. The terrified anglers said that the animal also made a strange sound. Could the monster have been warning them, or perhaps it was tired of isolation and was trying to make contact?

More than three decades later, two separate groups of boaters described a three-humped creature that was 40 to 50 feet long. On a calm, overcast day in September 1994, the extremely still water suddenly rippled from the force of the monster's back breaking the surface. Witnesses say they observed the phenomenon for at least three minutes before it swam under their boats and disappeared.

In July 1996, people at different places on the lakeshore witnessed something about 20 feet long with several humps swim about 50 yards from shore. One sighting took place at 4 PM and another account was given by witnesses three hours later some 10 miles away. Those were just 2 of 10 sightings that year.

Is Memphré myth or reality? Are observers having optical illusions or do mysterious unknown creatures inhabit this Québec lake? Many experts in cryptozoology (the study of hidden animals) say that the evidence worldwide supports the existence of these unusual underwater animals.

Historian, monster enthusiast and scuba diver Jacques Boisvert has devoted more than 20 years to the search for a truthful answer. After nearly 5000 dives to his credit, he still has not seen the animal that he believes to live in Lake

Memphrémagog—though he thinks he may have stepped on one while scuba diving. On his website devoted to Memphré, Boisvert describes a time when he put his hand down on what he thought was a tree stump. When the "stump" felt his touch, it took off in a cloud of mud, leaving the diver trying to catch his breath.

"I couldn't say that it definitely was Memphré because I didn't see it. It could have been anything or it could have been his tail," comments Boisvert.

According to the British Columbia Scientific Cryptozoology Club, Barbara Malloy holds the distinction of photographing the Memphrémagog animal twice and having seen it three times. Her photos show a single mountainous hump above the water. Ms. Malloy has joined forces with Jacques Boisvert in the search for Memphré, and they still hope to find definitive proof of the sea monster's existence. Their search got a boost in 1997 when Patricia de Broin Fournier captured video images of a strange animal creating waves as it frolicked in the lake. Apparently, the object in the video, however, did not have the usual serpentine form normally seen by witnesses, and many felt the shape could simply have been a large wave.

Whether you believe in sea monsters or not, this is one lake where you might do well to bear in mind the stories of all who say Memphré is more than a myth.

Champie, the Monster of Lake Champlain

LAKE CHAMPLAIN

Not far down the road from Lake Memphrémagog is Lake Champlain, which borders Québec, New York and Vermont. In cryptozoological terms, it would seem that this lake is a fertile territory for lake monsters. The legend of the Lake Champlain monster, known as "Champ" or "Champie," has been around for more than 400 years, and whether it is some surviving prehistoric creature or just a work of fiction remains debatable. At least one photograph stands as possible evidence that something mysterious lives in the cold, deep water.

Champ is usually described as having a long neck and a flat head with a body that ranges from 10 to 30 feet long. Native tradition asserts the presence of a water monster in the lake. The Iroquois on the western side of the lake and the Abanaki and Algonquin on the east each have their own stories of a horned serpent that the Abanaki called Tatoskok. French explorer Samuel de Champlain encountered the lake in 1609, and for years accounts existed that he also encountered the beast; however, historians debunked that myth. While Champlain did report seeing a monstrous creature in the lake, evidence suggests that it may have been a garpike or a sturgeon. His "sighting" nonetheless became the first of a trend that continues to this day.

As the area became more populated with white settlers in the 1800s, the number of sightings increased dramatically with reports coming in nearly every year. In 1819, witnesses in Bulwagga Bay, near Port Henry, New York, claimed to see something swimming in the dark waters. In 1871, holiday-makers on board the steamship *Curlew* were enjoying the scenery of Horseshoe Bay when they were startled by the sight of a long-necked, horse-headed creature with several humps trailing behind its fore-section and with a wake 30 to 40 feet long. Two years later, railway workers laying track near Dresden, New York, saw the head of an "enormous serpent" emerge from Lake Champlain. According to a *New York Times* article, the spectacle paralyzed the men with shock, but they quickly recovered and ran away, and the creature swam off. Witnesses described the animal as having bright silver scales that glistened in the sun. "The appearance of his head was round and flat, with a hood spreading out from the lower part of it like a rubber cap often worn by mariners." That same year, a small steamship loaded with tourists allegedly struck the creature and nearly overturned. Newspaper accounts stated that the head and neck of the animal were sighted afterward about 100 feet from the ship.

As Champ's fame—or infamy—grew, so did interest in catching him. Showman P.T. Barnum offered a $50,000 reward for the person who could bring him the great serpent to add to his travelling World's Fair Show. But for the remainder of the 19th century, only reports of sightings of a colossal sea serpent came in, with sources ranging from a county sheriff to a group of picnickers.

Modern times have produced yet more reports of a long serpent with an arched back and broad, flat tail. In 1970, two independent witnesses travelling on a ferry across the lake spotted the creature. Richard Spear said the animal was "dark brownish-olive" in colour and "the size and shape of a barrel in cross-section." The other witness said that the aquatic curiosity appeared to be "a large snakelike creature, swimming with its head above water, held as snakes do, with coils behind."

The descriptions inspired many experts to believe that the animal might be a surviving plesiosaur. Plesiosaurs were marine reptiles with long necks, bulky bodies, four fins and a long tail. They have been thought extinct since the dinosaur age ended some 65 million years ago.

New York schoolteacher Joseph Zarzynski took such an interest in Champ that he formed the Lake Champlain Phenomena Investigation (LCPI) in the 1970s. His group organized observations of the lake, exploring its depths with sonar and even a small robotic submarine. The subsurface scans turned up some interesting blips but provided no conclusive proof that the elusive beast lives in the lake.

Sandra Mansi has the distinction of capturing on film the clearest evidence to date of any lake monster, not just in Lake Champlain but worldwide. The so-called "Mansi photograph" (copyrighted by its owner) came out of a summer picnic by the lake on July 5, 1977. Sandra and her husband, Anthony, had been visiting relatives in Vermont and stopped at the lake to let their two children run and play. Suddenly, the idyllic tranquillity dissolved as the shocked family watched a huge blackish-grey animal rise from the depths as if a submarine was breaking the surface. Anthony bundled up his children and ran for the car; Sandra hastily snapped a photo. The image—kept a secret by the family for three years for fear of ridicule—reveals what appears to be the neck and back of a large creature. The huge animal has a small head, long neck and humped back, and resembles something prehistoric.

Highly contested by experts, the picture is still the most famous image of Champie, and analysis by both the Smithsonian Institution and the University of Arizona's optical sciences department has failed to discredit the photograph. British Columbia expert Paul LeBlond estimated from the surrounding waves that the object in the picture was between 24 and 78 feet in length, which is much higher than Mansi's estimate of 15 to 20 feet.

In 1981 cryptozoologist Roy Mackal suggested that the creature might be a surviving zeuglodon (also known as a basilosaurus), a primitive form of whale with a long snake-like body that would match many of the reported descriptions but not the Mansi photograph. The fossils of such a creature were found near Charlotte, Vermont, just a few miles from Lake Champlain. Others, such as current researcher Dennis Jay Hall, have postulated that it is a tatystropheus, a long-necked reptile similar to a plesiosaur.

Is there really a Champ? Skeptics point out that if monsters have been surviving in Lake Champlain, there must be enough to have a breeding population. Could that many large lake monsters live there and be spotted only rarely? Those who question Champ's existence say it is unlikely. Scientists offer another possible explanation based on the lake's formation. Lake Champlain resembles Loch Ness in that both are long, narrow and cold, with an underwater wave called a *seiche* that can throw debris from the bottom of the lake to the surface. Some think this may explain many of the monster sightings.

But others, such as Dennis Hall, who heads Champ Quest, believe there is a mystery in the lake. Hall claims to have new video evidence that proves the existence of "large unidentified animals in Lake Champlain." After studying the incidents for 20 years, Hall predicts that sightings will occur within five days before and after the new moon. He claims more than 19 sightings and has a 75 percent success rate in his predictions. Whether all these ongoing efforts are successful in unmasking the true identity of the mysterious Champ remains to be seen.

The End